Hot Pink Dress

by Judy Ross

Everyone wants a hot pink dress. Make your own with this dress pattern and hot pink ribbon. Add some tags and it's "charming".

MATERIALS: Linen Diamond paper • Linen Tags stickers • Cardstock: Antique White, Black • Ribbon: 1½" wide Hot Pink, ½" Black and White • Clear crystal rhinestone • 5 small Gold safety pins • Bead trimming • *Ranger* Gold Ice Stickles • Fabri-Tac adhesive • Craft knife • Foam tape • Glue

INSTRUCTIONS:
Cut Antique White cardstock 7" x 10". Fold to 5" x 7". • Cut Diamond paper 4½" x 6". Adhere to card. • Cut Black cardstock 4¼" x 5½". • Trace dress pattern on Black cardstock. • Cut slits at the top, bottom and just around waist on both sides. • Slide 4½" of Hot Pink ribbon through the slits. Tuck into sides. Allow to pucker so you can get the dimension. • Glue beading to bottom of the Black cardstock. Attach to card with foam tape. • Spell "Charm" with tags. Add Gold safety pins and bows. • Highlight shape of dress with Ice Stickles.

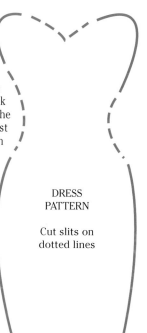

DRESS PATTERN

Cut slits on dotted lines

I Love U Card

by Judy Ross

If you love him, tell him so. Don't wait for a special day to send this fun card.

MATERIALS: Linen Stripe paper • Cardstock: Black, Pink • Stickers: Linen Tags, Black White Words • 2¾" Black mini file folder • 2 clear clothespins • Pink and Black Polka Dot ribbon • Black metallic thread • ¾" heart hole punch • Foam tape • Glue stick

INSTRUCTIONS:
Cut Black cardstock 5½" x 8½". Fold to 4¼" x 5½". • Cover with 4¼" x 5½" Linen Stripe paper. • Cut Pink cardstock 3" x 4". • Wrap file folder with ribbon and tie. • Adhere "love" sticker on file folder. • Tie tags with thread. Adhere to file folder with foam tape. • Punch 3 Pink hearts and mount to folder with foam tape. • Use clothespins to attach folder to Pink cardstock. • Attach Pink cardstock to card with foam tape. • Wrap with Black metallic thread.

Dove Card

by Karen Wells
Loving doves deliver this perfectly pink Valentine. Everyone will want this one!

MATERIALS: Baby Stripes paper • Cardstock: Light Pink, Dark Pink • Valentine stickers • Aqua square brads • ⅛" hole punch • Glue

INSTRUCTIONS:
Cut Dark Pink cardstock 7" x 10". Fold to 5" x 7". • Cut Light Pink cardstock 4½" x 6½". • Cut Baby Stripes paper 4" x 6". Adhere to Light Pink paper. • Affix dove sticker. • Punch holes in corners of Light Pink paper. • Attach colored brads. Glue Light Pink paper to card.

Valentine Love Card

by Karen Wells
So simple, so delightful, so loving. A hand-made card is a gift of your creativity and caring.

MATERIALS: Baby Stripes paper • Pink cardstock • Valentine stickers • Victorian slide mount • ¼" wide sheer Pink ribbon • Pink brads • Metal charm • ⅛" hole punch • Glue

INSTRUCTIONS:
Cut Pink cardstock 7" x 10". Fold to 5" x 7". • Cut Baby Stripes paper 4" x 4". Adhere to card. • Wrap Pink ribbon on side of slide mount and tie with metal charm. • Attach sticker to Baby Stripes paper and glue the slide mount over the sticker. • Punch holes in "Love" sticker and attach brads. Apply sticker to card.

Ice Cream Cone Card

by Molly Jennings
Turn a whimsical paper into a fantastic card by creating bottle cap embellishments to match.

MATERIALS: Cardstock: Tan, White, Pink • *NRN Designs* Ice Cream Cone paper • 2 Gold Bottle Caps • Brown watercolor pencil • Raffia • Acrylic paint: White, Green, Brown, Pink • Clear enamel spray • Small paintbrush • Glue • Foam dots

INSTRUCTIONS:
Bottle Caps: Flatten 2 bottle caps. Paint caps with 2 coats of White. Let dry. • Paint 1 cap Pink. Paint the other cap Green with tiny Brown "chips." Let dry. • Lightly spray with clear enamel. • **Card**: Cut Tan cardstock 5½" x 8½". Fold card to 4¼" x 5½". • Cut an Ice Cream Cone paper mat 3¼" x 4½". Cut a Pink mat 2" x 3¾". Cut a White mat 1¾" x 3½". Glue the mats in place. • **Accent**: Cut a Tan scrap into a cone shape. Draw waffle lines on the cone with a watercolor pencil, then go over them with wet brush. Glue the cone to the card. • Affix the bottle caps to the card with a foam dots under the top cap. • Add a raffia bow.

Door Hanger

by Wendy Malichio

Let the romantic atmosphere begin at the door with a Vintage Valentine door hanger. Roses, doves and classic colors invite your guests to celebrate the season of love.

MATERIALS: Paper: Linen Diamond, Linen Stripe • Black cardstock • Gold Bottle Cap • Stickers: Valentine, Vintage Faces • Heavy cardboard • *Ranger* Black Soot Distress ink • ½" wide sheer Red ribbon

INSTRUCTIONS:
Using pattern, trace and cut out door hanger from heavy cardboard and Black cardstock. • Adhere Black stripe in Linen Stripe paper to front of door hanger. • Adhere Linen Diamond paper to the lower 5½" of the hanger. • Ink the edges of the door hanger and stickers. Let dry. • Wrap ribbon around the hanger along the top edge of the Linen Diamond paper. • Apply stickers, ribbons, and bottle cap with Rose sticker. • Cover back of hanger with Black cardstock.

PATTERN | ←   Place on fold

Vintage Valentine

by Wendy Malichio

Love is a collage of feelings! Express that special mix with a Vintage Valentine's card combining an assortment of fibers, metals and papers.

MATERIALS: Papers: Linen Vine, Linen Diamond • *Bazzill* Pinecone cardstock • Black Bottle Cap • Stickers: Valentine, Vintage Faces, Linen Tags • Brads • Ribbon: ½" wide sheer Red, ⅜" wide Black and White Check • 3" x 4" White fabric scrap • *Ranger* Nick Bantock Van Dyke Brown ink • Staples • E6000 adhesive • Glue stick

INSTRUCTIONS:
Cut Pinecone cardstock 7" x 11". Fold to 5½" x 7". • Cut Linen Vine paper 5" x 6½". Ink the edges. • Cut Linen Diamond paper 1¾" x 6¾". Ink the edges. • Position Diamond strip over the Vine paper. Wrap ribbon around papers. Secure ribbon with staples. • Position fabric. • Attach Check ribbon to vintage sticker with heart brad. • Apply Valentine stickers over fabric. • Apply letter stickers. Attach brads. • Adhere Linen Vine paper to card with glue stick. • Flatten the bottle cap and adhere sticker. • Adhere to card with E6000.

Red Valentine's Card

by Karen Wells

Red is the color of passion. Line the inside of this simple card with a white paper or parchment and scribe your message with feeling.

MATERIALS: Red cardstock • Valentine stickers • 2 White metal clips • ⅛" wide Red ribbon • 3½" x 4¼" fabric • Xyron adhesive • The Ultimate! Glue • Tape

INSTRUCTIONS:
Cut Red cardstock 6¼" x 9". Fold to 4½" x 6¼". • Attach the fabric to card with Xyron adhesive. • Apply sticker to fabric. •Attach metal clips to sides of heart sticker. • Glue the metal clips to card. • Thread ribbon through metal clips. • Tape ribbon ends inside the card.

Joyous Day Card
by Janet Hopkins

Live it up when you can and have a joyous day! Send this card to someone who needs a little lift and you will make their day.

MATERIALS: *Bazzill* cardstock: Teal, Leapfrog • Large Metal Disk • Spring Flowers Postcards Sticker • ¾" wide ribbon • Ecru paint • Rub-ons • *Ranger* Nick Bantock Van Dyke Brown ink • Sandpaper • *JudiKins* Diamond Glaze • E6000 adhesive

INSTRUCTIONS:
Cut Teal cardstock 4¾" x 12". Score a fold 3" from each end. • Sew ribbon to the front edge of each card flap. • Lightly paint metal disk. Let dry. • Ink over the painted disk. Let dry. Sand lightly. • Cut "Joyous Day" sticker to fit the disk. Ink the edges. • Adhere sticker to metal disk. • Fill disk with Diamond Glaze. Let dry for 24 hours. • Cut 2 pieces of Leapfrog cardstock 3" x 4¾". Adhere inside each flap to cover the sewing. • Apply rub-on words "Live it up when you can" inside card. • Use E6000 to adhere only half of the metal disk to the right side of card so card will still open.

Paris in the Spring
by Lisa Vollrath

There is no place I would rather be than Paris. It is even better in the Spring. Make a card that takes you there!

MATERIALS: Vintage Bottle Cap paper • Cardstock: Red, Hunter Green • Large Metal Disk • Stickers: Vintage Children, Spring Flowers Postcards • Eiffel Tower postcard or photo • Clear acrylic button cover • Heart-shaped sequins • Pin back • 2" twill tape • Letter stamps • Butterscotch acrylic • Black dye ink • ½" heart punch • Foam squares • E6000 adhesive

INSTRUCTIONS:
Cut Hunter cardstock 6" x 12". Fold to 6" x 6". • Cut Vintage Bottle Cap paper 5¾" x 5¾" and glue it to center front of card. • Paint rim of metal disk with Butterscotch acrylic. Let dry. • Cut a 2½" circle from Eiffel Tower photo. • Stamp "I" with Black dye ink. • Punch a small Red cardstock heart. Glue it beside the "I". • Attach "Paris" sticker to photo. Pile sequins in center of photo. • Apply a bead of E6000 to the edge of button and place on photo. • Let dry completely before moving. • Attach pin back to back of lid. • Attach foam squares to postcard stickers and adhere to card. • Glue twill tape to front of card. Let dry. • Pin through twill tape to attach pin to front of card.

Mother's Day
by Wendy Malichio

Tell Mom how special she is with a vintage card made uniquely for her.

MATERIALS: 2 sheets da Vinci Script paper • *Bazzill* cardstock: Fawn, Olive • Large Metal Disk; Spring Flowers Postcards Sticker • *Ranger* Nick Bantock Van Dyke Brown ink • ⅜" wide Black and White ribbon • E6000 adhesive • Glue stick

INSTRUCTIONS:
Cut Fawn cardstock 6" x 11". Fold to 5½" x 6". Ink the edges. • Cut Olive cardstock 2⅛" x 5". Ink the edges. Glue to card. • Cut da Vinci paper 4¾" x 6" so the face is in the upper right corner. • Tear ½" off the bottom edge. Ink the edges. Adhere to card. • Ink the edge of the sticker. • Wrap ribbon around the sticker and tie a knot. • Adhere sticker and ribbon to card. • Cut face image from second sheet of da Vinci paper to fit the metal disk. Ink the edge. • Adhere face image to disk. Adhere disk over face on card with E6000.

1. 2. 3. 4.

5. 6. 7. 8.

Metal Disk Accents

Now you can make exciting, one-of-a-kind accents for gift tags, gift boxes, scrapbook pages and cards. Check out these neat ideas and let your imagination run wild.

9.

• 1. Cut 2 circles from paper. Tear one circle in half raggedly. Glue to second circle. Edge with chalk inkpad. Glue silk ribbon across circle. Glue to metal disk. Tie a silk ribbon bow and glue to disk. Apply letter with foam dots.

• 2. Cut a paper circle and edge with chalk ink. Glue to metal disk. Dab edges of circle with glue and apply micro beads. Use label maker to write words.

• 3. Paint metal disk with metallic acrylics and let dry. Cut a paper circle and edge with chalk ink. Glue to ___ disk. Flatten bottle cap, decorate with sticker, and ap___ disk with foam square. Edge word sticker with chalk an___ pply to disk with foam dots.

• 4. Cut a paper circle and edge with chalk inks. Glue to metal disk. Cut heart from cardstock. Glue strip of silk ribbon across heart. Decorate with metal letters and small buttons. Attach to metal disk with foam dots.

• 5. Paint metal disk with acrylic paints. Cut a paper circle and edge with chalk inks. Pile star sequins in center of paper circle, and glue top of button to paper. Let set until completely dry. Glue to metal disk.

• 6. Paint metal disk with gesso. While still wet, cut circle from transparency sheet and place in center of disk. Let dry. Dab with glitter glue to add sparkle.

• 7. Cut circle from photo and apply to metal disk. Apply word sticker and star sequin to photo with foam dots.

• 8. Cut photo and apply to metal disk. Tear small piece of mulberry paper and glue over edge of photo. Drill holes in bottom of disk and hang letter charms with jump rings. Adhere metal letters to mulberry paper.

• 9. Cut out paper circle. Ink the edges. Decorate as desired.

• 10. Drill holes in metal disk for charms and hangers. Paint with Gold metallic paint and let dry. Cut circle from photo and apply to disk. Hang charms and beads from eye pins. Thread ribbon through jump rings and attach to top of disk. Hang from decorative button.

10.

11.

• 11. Drill hole in metal disk and thread with fibers. Apply rub-on to metal disk. Age small envelope with chalk inks and stamp as desired.

• 12. Drill holes through five metal disks. Paint with metallic acrylics. Let dry. Thread split ring through holes. Cut circles from photos and glue to disks. Decorate with word stickers.

12.

Valentine Clown

by Wendy Malichio

People of all ages love receiving cards. Send some-one a smile with this Vintage Valentine Clown.

MATERIALS: da Vinci Diamond paper • *Bazzill* Vanilla cardstock • Stickers: Vintage Faces, Valentine, Black White Words • Orange Bottle Cap • ¼" ribbon • Staples

INSTRUCTIONS:
Cut cardstock 7¼" x 11". Fold to 5½" x 7¼". • Trim da Vinci Diamond paper 3¼" x 6". • Staple ribbon to Diamond paper. Adhere to card. • Add "beloved" and Valentine stickers. • Flatten bottle cap. Apply face sticker and adhere to card with E6000.

Valentine Pin

by Karen Wells

Cupid comes in many disguises. Here, the Harlequin of Love offers a traditional red heart to your favorite Valentine. This card comes with a detachable, wearable pin.

MATERIALS: Cardstock: Tan, Red • Small Metal Disk • Stickers: Valentine Postcards, Vintage Faces • Buttons • ¼" Ribbon • Metal letters • Pin back • E6000 adhesive

INSTRUCTIONS:
Card: Cut Tan cardstock 5½" x 8½". Fold to 4¼" x 5½". • Cut Red cardstock 2⅝" x 3½". • Adhere ribbon and Valentine sticker to card.
Pin: Cut sticker of boy to fit and adhere to the metal disk. • Glue buttons around the rim of the disk with E6000. • Glue letters inside tag and adhere pin back with E6000. • Cut 2 vertical slits in Red cardstock and attach pin. • Affix the Red cardstock to the front of card with butterfly stickers.

Love Card

by Wendy Malichio

Celebrate the most romantic holiday of the year with a lovely vintage card.

MATERIALS: Linen Diamond paper • *Bazzill* Marina cardstock • Stickers: Valentine Postcards, Linen ABC Tags • Brads • Ribbon • Glue stick

INSTRUCTIONS:
Cut Marina cardstock 5¼" x 11". • Tear one end to 5¼" x 10". • Fold to 5" x 5¼". • Add stickers, brads and ribbon. • Cut Linen Diamond paper 1¼" x 5¼". • Fold to ¾" x 5¼". Align the fold with the card fold. • Glue Linen Diamond paper to the top of the card.

Dear Mother

by Wendy Malichio

Tell Mom what a blessing she is and how much you appreciate all she has done with the collage card.

MATERIALS: *Bazzill* cardstock: Moss, Stucco • Stickers: Vintage Faces, Spring Flowers Postcards, Coffee Words • Gold Bottle Cap • Ribbon • *Ranger* Vintage Photo Distress ink • Glue

INSTRUCTIONS:
Cut Moss cardstock 6¼" x 8½". Fold to 4¼" x 6¼". • Ink the edges to distress the card. • Cut Stucco cardstock 2" x 3". Ink the edges. • Wrap ribbon around the Stucco strip. • Adhere "Dear Mother" and "blessing" stickers. • Flatten a bottle cap, apply a face sticker, adhere to card.

Mom's Box

by Wendy Malichio

Decorative boxes have been popular since Victorian times. This small tin is perfect to carry change in the car, small items in a purse, or on a dresser to hold earrings.

MATERIALS: Small tin • da Vinci Diamond paper • Spring Flowers Postcards sticker • Metal Letter • ¼" wide ribbon • *Ranger* Black Soot Distress ink • Sandpaper • Gesso • Glue

INSTRUCTIONS:
Sand tin, then paint a layer of gesso. • Sand tin again when dry so parts of the tin show through.• Adhere da Vinci Diamond paper and sticker to the lid. • Ink the tin. Let dry. • Glue ribbon to the lid. • Adhere metal "M" for mom.

Precious Baby Face

by Molly Jennings

Welcome the newest addition to the family with a precious card.

MATERIALS: Pink A-Z paper • *Bazzill* cardstock: White, Petunia • Stickers: Fun Faces, Pink Words • Pink metal clip • White Bottle Cap • ¼" Pink satin ribbon • Yellow embroidery floss • Foam tape • Goop adhesive • Glue stick

INSTRUCTIONS:
Cut White cardstock 5½" x 8½". Fold to 4¼" x 5½". • Flatten bottle cap. Adhere floss, fun face sticker, and ribbon. • Cut Petunia cardstock 2⅝" x 2⅞". • Cut Pink A-Z paper 2¼" x 2½". • Adhere A-Z paper to cardstock. Glue bottle cap in place. • Attach clip and mount panel to card with foam tape. Apply word sticker.

Handprints Card

by Molly Jennings

Delicate pink papers and ribbons make this beautiful baby card perfect for the arrival of your princess.

MATERIALS: Pink A-Z paper • *Bazzill* cardstock: Baby Pink, White • 2 Pink Bottle Caps • Girl Pink Sayings stickers • Gold thin cord • ⅝" Pink ribbon

INSTRUCTIONS:
Cut Pink cardstock 5½" x 8½". Fold to 4¼" x 5½". • Cut White cardstock 2⅝" x 3⅜". Adhere to card. • Cut A-Z paper 2½" x 3¼". Adhere to card. • Knot Gold cord to create a loop at top. • Attach to card and place ribbon bow on top. • Flatten bottle caps and adhere handprint stickers to them. • Glue bottle caps over ends of Gold cord.

Posy Frame

by Molly Jennings

Small and simple, this frame is a nice size for your desk at work.

MATERIALS: Baby Stripes paper • 3" metal disk • 2 Pink metal clips • Tiny flowers and leaves • ⅛" Pink satin ribbon • Photo • White spray enamel paint • Glue stick • Goop adhesive

INSTRUCTIONS:
Spray both sides of metal disk with White enamel. Let dry. • Cut a 2¼" circle from Baby Stripes paper and adhere to White disk. • Trim photo as desired and glue in place over paper circle. • Attach clips to the bottom of the frame so it stands up. • Attach flowers around rim and on bottom of clips with Goop adhesive. • Add a bow.

Posy Pincushion

by Molly Jennings

Here's a fun project that you can complete in about an hour.

MATERIALS: White bottle cap • Needle • Thread • Fine White tulle netting • Tiny flowers and leaves • New steel wool • Cotton ball • Fabric • Goop adhesive

INSTRUCTIONS:
Cut a strip of netting approximately 1½" x 14" long. • Gather into circle by sewing large stitches along long edge. Knot securely. • Cut one 3¼" fabric circle. • Stitch along edge and pull stitches in to form a ball, leaving an opening for stuffing. • Roll 1" ball from a piece of steel wool and stuff inside. • Tuck in pieces of cotton for added fullness. • Pull stitches tightly and sew shut. • Glue net circle inside bottle cap, pushing net to edges. • Glue cloth ball onto netting, pushing for a snug fit. • Cover with fabric. Decorate with flowers and leaves.

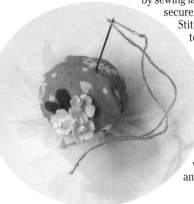

LARGE
POSY
PATTERN

Adorable Posy
by Molly Jennings
Fluff up a flower with a bit of tulle netting.

MATERIALS Papers: Pink Word Blocks, Baby Books • White bottle cap • 4¼" x 5½" folded White card • ¼" Pink satin ribbon • Needle • Fine White thread • Tulle netting • Punches: Small flower, 1" circle • Tiny pearl • Goop adhesive

INSTRUCTIONS:
Flatten bottle cap. Punch baby face from Baby Books paper. • Cut out a large flower from Pink Word Blocks paper. • Score centers of flower petals and bend petal edges upwards slightly. • Adhere large flower to card tucking ribbon stems under blossom. • Cut out "adorable" word, and punch a small flower from Pink Word Blocks paper. Adhere to card. Add bead. • Cut a strip of netting about 1½" x 26" and gather with needle and thread along long edge and pull into circular shape and secure thread. • Glue net circle and bottle cap to center of flower. • Adhere punched baby face to bottle cap. • Attach ribbon bow.

SMALL
POSY
PATTERN

Baby Buggy
by Molly Jennings
Looking for a unique accent? Try this baby buggy made from a metal disk.

MATERIALS: 5" x 7" folded White card • Pink Word Blocks paper • 2 White bottle caps • Large metal disk • Gold thick bendable wire • Pink ¼" ribbon • Spiral punch • Gesso paint • White acrylic paint • Paint brush • Clear enamel spray • Sturdy scissors • Goop adhesive • Glue stick

INSTRUCTIONS:
Carefully cut a wedge out of the metal disk with sturdy scissors. • Paint disk with 2 coats of gesso, followed by 2 coats of White acrylic paint. Let dry between all coats. • Spray with clear enamel and let dry. • Cut 4" x 5" rectangle of Pink Word Blocks paper. Adhere to card.
• Attach buggy and bottle cap wheels to card with Goop. • Punch 2 spirals from the same paper and adhere to wheels.
• Bend wire into handle shape and glue in place. Add bow.

Sweet Onesie

by Molly Jennings

Create a cute accent from a piece of white fabric. This onesie is a simple cut-out.

MATERIALS: 5" x 7" White card • Girl Pink paper • White cardstock • 2 Pink clothespins • Girl Sayings stickers • White cotton fabric • White paper scrap • Gold thin metallic ribbon • ⅛" hole punch • Tacky craft glue • Glue stick

INSTRUCTIONS:
Cut White cardstock 4¾" x 6¼". • Cut Girl Pink paper 4⅜" x 6" (3 rows by 4 rows). Adhere to White cardstock. • Punch ⅛" holes on bottle cap panel. • Thread Gold ribbon through holes as clothesline and secure to back of panel. Adhere panel to card. • Lightly trace onesie with pencil on White fabric and on White paper. • Apply a thin line of White glue around pencil outline on fabric onesie tracing to stiffen. Let dry. • Cut out both onesies. Trim the paper one inside the pencil line. • Layer fabric over paper onesie. Adhere at neck edges with glue stick. • Clip cloth and paperbacked onesie to clothesline with Pink clothespins.
• Adhere sticker on onesie.

ONESIE
PATTERN

It's A Girl

by Janet Hopkins

Apply rub-ons to flattened bottle caps for a great title. The pacifier charm and ribbon add that special touch to this fun accent.

MATERIALS: Girl Pink paper • Pink card • 3 White Bottle Caps • Ribbon • Pink paint • Rub-ons • Pacifier charm • Foam dots

INSTRUCTIONS:
Cut a 4¼" square Girl Pink paper. • Sew a zig zag stitch ¼" from the edges.• Paint the edges of the Girl Pink paper and card. • Adhere stitched Girl Pink paper to the front of the card. • Flatten bottle caps. Adhere rub-ons. Distress with Pink paint. • In the middle bottle cap, punch 2 holes. • Thread ribbon through holes and tie charm. • Adhere the bottle caps in place.

Baby Love

by Wendy Malichio

There are many ways to decorate bottle caps. Apply stickers, or add pebble letters.

MATERIALS: Baby Stripes paper • *Bazzill* cardstock: White, Baby Pink • 4 Silver Bottle Caps • Stickers: Baby Milestones, Black White Words • Pebble Letter Stickers • Ribbon • Punches: 1" circle, corner rounder • *Ranger* Black Soot Distress ink

INSTRUCTIONS:
Cut White cardstock 6" x 11". Fold to 5½" x 6". Ink the edges. • Cut 3 Baby Stripes rectangles 2" x 4¾". • Punch the corners. Ink the edges. • Tie a ribbon around one of the rectangles. Add stickers. • Adhere to card. • Punch and ink Pink circles. Adhere to bottle caps. • Add letter pebbles to bottle caps and adhere to card.

You're Invited

by Diana McMillan

Next time you need to make several invitations, remember this simple one.

MATERIALS: Baby Stripes paper • White cardstock • Stickers: Girl Sayings, Baby Milestones • Pink Bottle Cap • *McGill* Buttonhole punch • Pink sheer ribbon • Foam Squares • Memory Tape Runner

INSTRUCTIONS:
Cut White cardstock and Baby Stripes paper 3¾" x 5¼".
• Adhere paper to cardstock.
• Apply sticker. • Flatten the bottle cap. Apply sticker.
• Punch hole in the top of the invitation. • Thread ribbon through holes. • Adhere bottle cap in place with foam squares.

Thank You Tag

Here's a beautiful way to say "thanks".

MATERIALS: Baby Stripes paper • Pink Tag ABCs sticker • White cardstock • Pink brad • Pink ribbon • *ColorBox* Cat's Eye Pink ink • Black pen • Foam Squares, • Memory Tape Runner

INSTRUCTIONS:
Cut White cardstock 2½" x 5½". Fold to 2½" x 2½". • Cut Baby Stripes paper 2½" x 3¾". Adhere to cardstock. • Make a Pink ribbon bow. Glue over ribbon on paper. • Ink the edges of the "T" tag. • Insert Pink brad through tag. • Adhere tag to card with foam squares. • Write "Thank You!"

Gift Box & Tag

Pretty papers form this attractive handmade box. Wrap it with a ribbon and a tag for that perfect finishing touch.

Gift Box:
MATERIALS: Papers: Baby Bubbles Pink, Baby Stripes • Pink Bottle Cap • Stickers: Girl Sayings, Pink Words • Pink clothespin • 1⅜" x 2⅞" manila tag • 1 yard 1½" wide Pink sheer ribbon • Double-sided tape • Glue
INSTRUCTIONS:

Tag:
Cover tag with Baby Stripes paper. • Cut 10" of ribbon. Tie a bow. Glue to back of tag. • Flatten bottle cap. Adhere to tag. Apply stickers. • Attach tag to ribbon on box with clothespin.

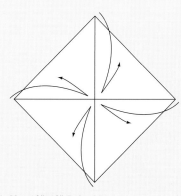

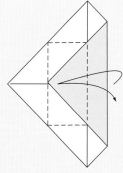

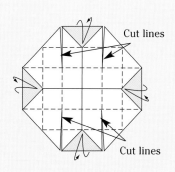

1. Use 12"x12" Baby Milestones paper for lid and cut one 11¾" Baby Stripes paper for bottom. Draw lines connecting corners on back side as shown. Fold four corners to center and unfold.

2. Fold in each of four corners with point to farthest fold line and unfold.

3. Cut on fold lines as indicated above and fold four corners to outer fold lines, then fold to reverse.

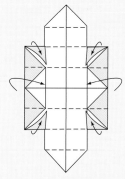

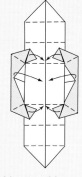

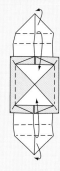

4. Fold in left and right sides as shown.

5. Fold top and bottom portions of sides as shown and bring to center.

6. Fold top and bottom sides in as shown.

7. Inside of finished box. Tape flaps down with double-sided tape.

Announcement

by Wendy Malichio

Personalize a baby announcement by adding a photo.

MATERIALS: Baby Stripes paper • Cardstock: Kraft, White • Kraft mini file folder • Stickers: Black White Words, Baby Milestones • White wire clip • *Dymo* Label Maker • *Ranger* ink • Ribbon • Border Punch • Safety pins • Staples • Glue stick

INSTRUCTIONS:
Computer print baby statistics on a sheet of White cardstock. • Cut Kraft cardstock 8½" x 12". Fold to 6" x 8½". • Cut Baby Stripes paper 4¾" x 6". • Punch the top with a decorative border. Ink the edges. • Pin a ribbon to the lower corner. Adhere to card. • Adhere photo. Staple ribbons in place. Add Dymo labels. • Add a safety pin to the top of the card. Tie ribbon to pin. • Ink the edges of the folder. Add label and stickers. • Place "baby stats" in folder and adhere to card. Add clip.

Our Baby

by Sherelle Christensen

Write the statistics for your bundle of joy in this book. Send it out as a baby announcement or add it to a scrapbook page.

MATERIALS: Baby Books paper • Kraft cardstock • Pink wire clip • Batting • Safety pin • Vintage ribbon • Pinking shears • Glue

INSTRUCTIONS:
Cut Kraft cardstock 5" x 8". Fold to 4" x 5". • Cut out the "Story of Our Baby" from the Baby Books paper. • Cut batting with pinking shears 3½" x 4½". • Pin Baby Book paper to batting. Adhere batting to card. • Add Pink clip. • Adhere ribbon to the inside of card and tie a bow to close the card.

Congratulations

by Wendy Malichio

Use safety pins and a ribbon to create a unique closure.

MATERIALS: Papers: Baby Books, Baby Milestones • *Bazzill* Fawn cardstock • Silver Bottle Cap • Stickers: Art Words, Pink Words • Computer fonts: Times New Roman, *Two Peas in a Bucket* Inside Out • *Ranger* ink • Decorative scissors • Safety pins • Fabric • Glue stick

INSTRUCTIONS:
Cut Fawn cardstock 8½" x 11". Trim one 8½" edge with decorative scissors to 8½" x 10½". • Starting with the decorative edge, score and fold 2" and 7" from the edge. • Print the word "Congratulations" on top flap part of card. • Adhere a strip of ribbon next to the decorative edge. • Adhere Baby Milestones paper to the large flap. • Fray the edges of a 3" x 4" fabric. Adhere to large flap. • Cut baby image from Baby Books paper. Adhere over fabric. • Adhere bottle cap, stickers and baby image. • Ink card edges as desired. • Using 2 safety pins, attach to top flap and bottom part of card, add ribbon to keep card closed.

Baby Journal
by Karen Wells

Make a pretty accordion journal with beautiful baby papers.

MATERIALS: Papers: Baby Books, Baby Stripes • 4⅞" x 14" Blue Art Paper • Two 3⅝" x 5" matboards • *Ten Seconds Studio* (Aluminum metal, Tools: C33, CS3, C10) • Spackle • Acrylic paint: Sandstone, Territorial Beige • Lace ribbon • The Ultimate! glue

INSTRUCTIONS:
Cover: Cut metal 3⅝" x 5". • Form the border with a ball and cup tool. • Using the roller embossing tools, form additional borders. • Apply spackle to the back of the cover and let dry. • Paint metal with Sandstone and brush with Beige paint. • Glue journal cover to metal. Glue metal to matboard. • For back cover, cut Baby Stripes paper 3⅝" x 5" and glue to matboard.

Book: Accordion-fold the Blue paper into 4 sections. • Cut panels from Baby Books paper and glue to each page. • Attach to front and back covers. • Glue lace ribbon to border first and last page of book.

Baby's Gift Tin
by Karen Wells

Decorated tins are fun pieces of art that store little treasures.

MATERIALS: Baby Milestones paper • White Bottle Cap • Stickers: Vintage Faces, Baby Milestones • Wire clips: 2 White, 1 Blue • Baby photo • Acrylic paint: Sandstone, White • Green ribbons • 1" circle punch • The Ultimate! glue

INSTRUCTIONS:
Paint cover of tin with Sandstone and bottom of tin with White. Let dry. • Cut Baby Milestones paper to fit interior of tin and glue to lid. • Cut ribbons and glue onto lid. • Attach face sticker to bottle cap and glue on lid. • Cut sticker to fit inside of lid and adhere. • Punch out photo and adhere to bottle cap. Glue inside lid. • Glue clips inside tin and attach stickers.

Baby Joy Card

by Karen Wells

Crossed ribbons add design, texture, and color to this pretty card.

MATERIALS: Papers: Baby Milestones, Baby Books • Manila cardstock • White Bottle Cap • Boy Sayings sticker • Buttons • Ribbon words • Beige acrylic paint • Glue

INSTRUCTIONS:
Cut Manila cardstock 5" x 10". Fold to 5" square. • Cut Baby Milestones paper 4½" square. • Cut ribbon words to criss-cross Baby Milestones paper and glue in place, wrapping around the ends to the back of the paper. • Cut out image from Baby Books paper and glue to card. • Glue buttons in place. • Paint bottle cap Beige. Let dry. • Apply sticker and affix cap to card.

Baby Boy on Bubble

by Molly Jennings

Make a fun card to celebrate a baby boy.

MATERIALS: Papers: Baby Bubbles Pink, Baby Books, Baby Stripes • Victorian Blue slide mount with tag • 4¼" x 5½" folded Light Blue card • ⅛" gingham ribbon • *Hero Arts* tiny White button • Blue safety pin • Small lace doily • Glue

INSTRUCTIONS:
Cut baby and bubbles from Baby Bubbles paper. • Cut word "Baby" from Baby Books paper and attach to small Blue tag. • Cut Baby Stripes paper to fit slide mount. • Cut a piece of doily to fit inside mount as shown. • Assemble all as shown within slide mount. • Glue bow, pin, button, and paper bubbles in place.

Dear Father

by Molly Jennings

Give this card to Dad for a birthday or just to say "Thanks for all you do".

MATERIALS: Light Blue folded card 4¼" x 5½" • Spring Flowers Postcards stickers • Bottle Cap • Victorian Blue slide mount • Brown craft paper • *Tsukineko* Encore Ultimate Metallic Gold ink pad • 1" circle punch • Beads • Raffia • Glue

INSTRUCTIONS:
Lightly brush edges of card with Gold ink pad. • Place "Dear Father" sticker on cardstock scrap. • Tear Brown craft paper ½" x 3". Brush with Gold ink. Adhere to left side of sticker. • Attach this panel to the back of slide mount. • Tie raffia bow. Adhere to left side of slide mount. • Adhere mount to card. • Flatten bottle cap. • Punch out floral sticker and adhere inside bottle cap. • Adhere cap and beads to card.

Happy Birthday

by Janet Hopkins

Make this card easily with a pink bottle cap, a sticker, rub-ons and ribbon.

MATERIALS: White folded card • Pink Bottle Cap • Princess sticker • Ribbon • Jump ring * Rub-ons • Pink thread

INSTRUCTIONS:
Stitch a decorative border across the front of card with coordinating thread. • Flatten bottle cap and apply sticker. Adhere "happy" rub-on. • Tie ribbon around the front of card and tie in a knot. • Dangle the bottle cap from a jump ring on the ribbon. • Apply "birthday" rub-ons.

As Friends Go

by Mary Kaye Seckler

You're matchless! And so is this card. Check out this neat envelope!

MATERIALS: Two sheets Blue A-Z paper • 2 sheets Light Blue cardstock • Stickers: Citrus Brights, Blue ABCs, Road Trip ABC Tags • Bottle caps: 2 Blue, 2 White • Small Heidi Rub-Ons • Ribbons • ⅛" eyelets: 2 White, 4 Light Blue • *Doodlebug Designs:* Beetle Black Large, Flower buttons • Thread: Yellow, Blue • Box envelope template • *Tsukineko* Atlantic Versacolor cube • Drill • ⅛" drill bit • *Xyron* adhesive • Staples

CARD INSTRUCTIONS:
Cut a strip of Light Blue cardstock 4¼" x 12". • Score 1¼" from one end and fold. • Bring the other end ¼" under the folded flap and fold again to make a matchbook. • Attach "AS" stickers to top of front flap. • Set two Light Blue eyelets in the letters and two more above the letters. • Thread ribbons through eyelet pairs and tie a bow in each. • Add 'friends' rub-ons below 'as' stickers. • Flatten 2 Blue bottle caps and attach "GO" stickers. • Edge card with Atlantic ink. • Cut Blue A-Z paper 4¼" x 5". • Add "You're matchless" rub-ons. • Sew 3 Blue flower buttons with Yellow thread and 6 Green leaves with Green thread. • Insert Blue A-Z paper into matchbook and close the front flap. • Staple the Blue A-Z on the bottom flap, taking care not to catch the top flap in the staple.

BOX ENVELOPE INSTRUCTIONS:
Trace box envelope onto reverse side of Blue A-Z paper. • Cut out and run through Xyron machine. • Adhere Blue A-Z paper to cardstock and cut out again. • Lay template onto cardstock and score firmly along the lines. • Fold box envelope. • Flatten 2 White bottle caps. • Drill ⅛" holes in the center of two flat caps. • Add Citrus stickers to bottle cap tops and punch holes in stickers. • Punch a hole in one end of a piece of ribbon. • On the upper flap of the envelope, place the ribbon between the cap and envelope. Set an eyelet to secure ribbon and cap. • Set the other eyelet in the bottle cap on the bottom flap of the envelope. • Wrap ribbon around the bottle cap closure.

1. Score and fold 1¼" from the end.

2. Fold the other end to make a matchbook.

3. Edge with Blue ink.

4. Insert paper into matchbook and staple.

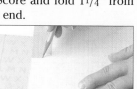

5. Trace envelope on reverse side of paper.

6. Cut out and adhere to cardstock.

7. Score and fold.

8. Attach bottle cap with eyelet.

Only You Card

by Janet Hopkins

This is a nice card to send someone who needs a lift. Make this one just to say, "I'm thinking of you".

MATERIALS: Pink A-Z paper • Pink Textured folded card • Pink wire clip • Pink Words stickers • Sandpaper • Glue stick

INSTRUCTIONS:
Cut Pink A-Z paper 3¾" x 5¾". • Sand the edges. Adhere to the front of the card. • Apply stickers. • Sand around the edges of the stickers. • Add Pink wire clip as the decorative closure for your card.

You Are Card

by Janet Hopkins

Don't wait for a special day to give someone a compliment. Make today a special day for someone with this sweet sentiment card.

MATERIALS: Pink Words stickers • Pink Textured folded card • Metal Flower Charm • Paint • White Rub-ons • White thread • Foam dots

INSTRUCTIONS:
Sew lines across the card as shown in photo. • Paint metal charm. Let dry. • Apply stickers, adhere flower charm, and add "You are" rub-ons to card.

Sweet
Little Angel

by Sherelle Christensen

This pretty card is definitely a gift from heaven. Celebrate your sweet little angel with this trifold card.

MATERIALS: Baby Books paper • Light Blue Cardstock • Pink check ribbon • Vintage Rose ribbon • Pens • Colored pencils • Tape

INSTRUCTIONS:
Cut cardstock 6¼" x 11". Fold each side into the center. • Add ribbon to each outer flap edge. • Tape 8" of ribbon inside each flap to create a closure. • Cut out baby image from Baby Books paper. Adhere to card. • Write the title "Sweet Little Angel".

Clothespin Card

by Karen Wells

Clothespins on a line make fun accents for a baby card. Combine them with stickers and bottle caps for a coordinated look.

MATERIALS: Papers: Baby Books, Baby Bubbles Blue • Blue cardstock • Stickers: Boy Sayings, Baby Milestones • 3 White Bottle Caps • 3 Blue clothespins • Ribbon • Photo mounts • Glue

INSTRUCTIONS:
Cut Blue cardstock 6¼" x 9". Fold to 4½" x 6¼". • Cut Baby Bubbles Blue paper 4" x 5¾". Adhere to card. • Glue clothespins to card. • Tie ends of ribbon and attach to clothespins. • Cut out image of baby. • Attach photo mounts behind the image and attach to clothespin. • Affix stickers to either side of image. • Apply stickers to bottle caps and glue to card.

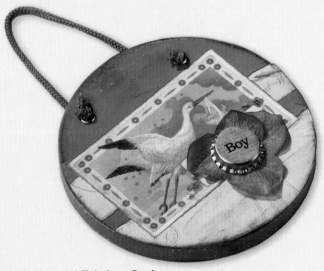

New Baby
Wall Hanging

by Wendy Malichio

Hang this one on the door to baby's room or enjoy it on the wall.

MATERIALS: Baby Milestones paper • Silver Bottle Cap • Stickers: Baby Milestones, Art Words • Paper Mache Hanging • Silk Flower • *Ranger* Vintage Photo Distress ink • Turquoise acrylic paint • Sandpaper • Goop adhesive

INSTRUCTIONS:
Paint the hanger. Let dry. • Sand lightly for a distressed look. • Tear Baby Milestones paper. Ink the edges. • Adhere inked paper, sticker, flower and bottle cap.

1. Punch circle.

2. Stamp letters.

3. Affix flat bottle cap to center.

4. Decorate with punched paper or sticker.

5. Glue ribbon to outer edges.

Proud Grandma

by Mary Kaye Seckler

We welcome into our world Jacob Allen Masterson. Ask me about Jake!

MATERIALS: Boy Blue paper • Cardstock: Light Blue, White • Stickers: Blue Alphabet, Boy Sayings • Blue bottle cap • 2⅜" metal disk • Blue ribbon • 1 self-adhesive pin back • *Hero Arts* Printer's Type rubber stamp alphabet • *Marvy* Blue pen • Computer font • Blue ink pad • Hole punches: 2" circle, fleur de lis corner, ⅛" circle • Glue dots • Glue stick

PIN INSTRUCTIONS:
Punch a 2" circle from the Light Blue cardstock. • Stamp 'Ask me about Jake' in a circle around the outside of the circle. • Flatten Blue bottle cap. Apply "100% Wonderful Boy" sticker. • Adhere bottle cap to center of Blue cardstock with a glue dot. • Affix Blue cardstock to disk with glue dots. • Tie knots in two shades of Blue ribbon and snip apart. • Attach ribbons to outer edge of disk with glue dots. • Adhere pin back to back of disk.

CARD INSTRUCTIONS:
Cut Blue cardstock to 7" x 7½". Fold to 3¾" x 7". • Apply stickers to front of card. • Use Blue pen to make the apostrophe in He's. • Punch two ⅛" holes about ¾" apart in the front panel of card. • Insert pin and close pin back. • Cut Boy Blue paper 3½" x 6¾" and adhere to inside left panel of card to cover pin back. • Computer print birth details in Champagne font on White cardstock. • Cut White cardstock 3" x 4". • Use fleur de lis corner punch on corners. Attach to inside right panel with glue dots.

Mini Book for Girls

by Janet Hopkins

Use these pages to collect signatures of friends, hold photos of boyfriends, and write your secret messages.

MATERIALS: Pink A-Z Word Blocks paper • *Bazzill* cardstock: Jubilee, Blush • Princess stickers • Pink Bottle Cap • Pink wire clip • Ribbon • 5½" x 9½" tags • *Ranger* Nick Bantock Charcoal Grey ink • Sandpaper • Glue • Double-sided Super Tape

INSTRUCTIONS:

Book: Cut Jubilee cardstock 6" x 12". Score 1" and 6¾" from one edge. Fold to make the mini book. Apply stickers to closing edge. • Cut Jubilee cardstock 3" x 5½". Accordion fold every ½" to make page holders.• Adhere the first folded section inside the cover, matching up the folds.

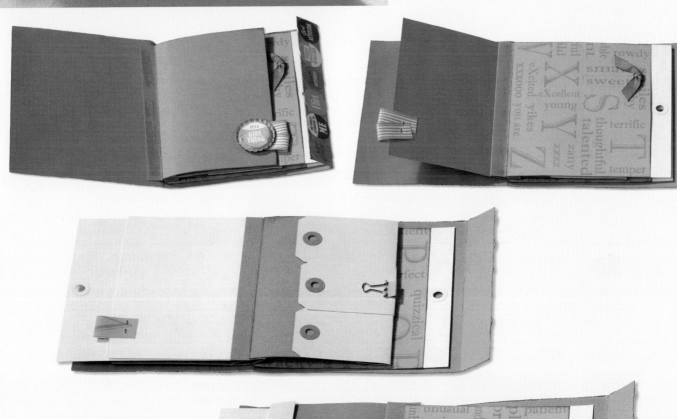

First Page:
Cut Jubilee cardstock 4" x 5½". • Ink and lightly sand the edges. • Lightly sand and ink sticker. Flatten the Pink bottle cap. Apply sticker. • Staple ribbon to page. Adhere bottle cap over staple. Glue page into fold of accordion.

Page 2:
Cut 5½" x 9½" tag into 2 pieces 5½" square and 4" x 5½". Cover the large piece with Pink A-Z Word Blocks paper and add a ribbon bow. Glue page into fold of accordion.

Page 3:
Make a tab for the small tag from Pink A-Z Word Blocks paper and staple in place. Glue page into fold of accordion.

Page 4:
Cut Jubilee cardstock 4" x 5½". Make 3 Pink tags from Blush cardstock 1¾" x 4". Wrap Pink tags around the page. Glue in place. Add a Pink clip.

Page 5:
Cut a 5½" square from the 5½" x 9½" tag. • Cover tag with Pink A-Z Word Blocks paper. Add a ribbon. Glue page into fold of accordion. • Tie a ribbon around the outside of the book to hold it together.

Birthday

by Janet Hopkins
Use this idea to personalize a window card.

MATERIALS: Pink A-Z Word Blocks paper • Open Windows Purple Card • Rub-ons:"Happy", "Birthday" • Ribbon • *Ranger* Nick Bantock Charcoal Grey ink • Sandpaper • Tape

INSTRUCTIONS:
Cut Pink A-Z Word Blocks paper to show through the window of the card. Tape in place. • Sand the outside of the card lightly for a distressed effect. Then ink the edges. • Punch 2 holes in the top right-hand corner of the large square for your ribbons. Thread through the hole and tie in a knot. • Apply rub-on words.

Mom

by Judy Ross
Remember Mother's Day with this nostalgic ribbons card.

MATERIALS: Linen Vine paper • Cardstock: Lilac, Green • White Bottle Caps • Typewriter Alphabet stickers • Lace fabric • 3 paper flowers • Lilac permanent ink • 25" Purple ribbon • Cosmetic sponge • Fabri-Tac glue

INSTRUCTIONS:
Cut Lilac cardstock 6" x 9½". Fold to 4¾" x 6". • Cut Green cardstock 4¼" x 5½" and glue to card.• Cut Linen Vine paper and lace 4½" x 6". • Glue lace over paper so the subtle vine shows through. • Wrap with ribbon. Glue to card. • Put stickers on caps and ink both caps and stickers. • Glue to card. • Glue flowers and make bows with remaining ribbon.

School Photo Holder
by Diana McMillan
Keep photos handy with this neat holder.

MATERIALS: Slide Mounts • Rollabind machine & disks • Glue

INSTRUCTIONS:
Punch holes in slide mounts with rollabind machine. • Adhere photos to mounts. • Adhere mounts back to back. • Attach slide mounts to disks.

Back to School
Make this fun card when your child or grandchild is just starting school.

MATERIALS: Papers: Black Chalkboard, School Books • Black cardstock • Stickers: School Days, Childhood Milestones • Red Bottle Cap • Red metal clip • 6" Red rickrack • Crayons • Small ruler • Vellum • Lemonade computer font • Foam Squares • Memory Tape Runner

INSTRUCTIONS:
Cut cardstock 5½" x 8½". Fold to 4¼" x 5½". • Cut 2 pieces of Black Chalkboard paper 5½" x 8½". • Adhere to front and inside of card.
OUTSIDE: Cut School Books paper 2¼" x 4¼" and adhere to bottom of the card. • Adhere rickrack to card. • Print "Back to school" on vellum and trim to fit. • Adhere metal clip to card. • Adhere Childhood Milestones sticker to bottom corner with foam squares.
INSIDE: Cut Black Chalkboard paper 4¼" x 5½". Trim diagonally from corner to corner. • Adhere Black Chalkboard triangles to inside cover on two sides to form pocket. • Adhere journal box sticker. • Flatten a bottle cap and add sticker. • Adhere cap to lower right corner of card with foam square. • Add crayons and ruler to inside pocket.

Graduation Card
by Molly Jennings
This happy card is a brilliant idea.

MATERIALS: Baby Stripes paper • 4¼" x 5½" folded White card • 4" square Black cardstock • White bottle cap • Stickers: Fun Faces, Black Words • Black wire clip • Yellow embroidery floss • ¼" Black ribbon • ¼" hole punch • Foam tape • Glue

INSTRUCTIONS:
Cut Black cardstock 2⅜" x 2⅝". Adhere to card. • Cut Baby Stripes paper 2⅛" x 2⅜". Adhere to card. • Flatten bottle cap and apply Fun Face sticker. Glue in place. • Cut diamond shape from Black cardstock for hat. • Punch tiny hole in center and thread floss through with knot at opposite end for tassel. • Glue floss across hat. Attach hat to top of head with foam tape. • Punch ¼" round circle from Black cardstock and glue to hat. • Add Black bow under chin and Black clip to top of card. • Attach "brilliant" sticker to card with foam tape.

Places You'll Go!
by Wendy Malichio
Celebrate the success of any graduate.

"PLACES" CARD PATTERN

MATERIALS: Road Trip Signs paper • Cardstock: White, Black • Silver Bottle Cap • Road Trip sticker • 2 Silver Metal Clips • *Ranger* Black Soot Distress ink • Computer Fonts • Glue stick

INSTRUCTIONS:
Using the pattern, cut octagon card from Black cardstock and smaller octagon from Road Trip Signs paper. • Adhere small octagon to front of card.• Print out "Oh The Places You'll Go". Ink and adhere to card using clips.• Add bottle cap with "One Way" sticker.

Place on fold

GRADUATION HAT PATTERN

Vacation Stationery Set

by Mary Kaye Seckler

Here's a fun way to make sure your kids write when they're away at camp. Custom design some cards and envelopes just for them decorated with license plates and coordinating stickers.

MATERIALS: Papers: Road Trip Map, 2 sheets Road Trip Black • Road Trip stickers • *Accu-Cut* card container die cut • Dark Brown cardstock • 2 sheets Kraft cardstock • 8 Kraft envelopes • 15" Ribbon • Silver buckle • 1 walnut ink dyed tag • 6" walnut ink dyed string • *Tsukineko* ink (Bark, Pinecone) • PVA glue • Glue stick

CARD AND ENVELOPE INSTRUCTIONS:
Cut 2 pieces of Kraft cardstock into quarters to make 8 cards measuring 4¼" x 5½". • Edge with Pinecone ink. • Apply Road Trip stickers to top right corners of cards. • Cut license plates out of scrapbook paper and adhere to envelope flaps with glue stick. • Edge flaps with Pinecone ink.

BOX INSTRUCTIONS:
Fold die cut along score lines and glue flaps together with PVA glue. • Cut Road Trip Black paper 5¼" x 9". Tear a ½" strip off each end and edge with Bark and Pinecone inks. Adhere to card container with glue stick.

TAG INSTRUCTIONS:
Cut out "Interstate 10" and "Route 1" labels from Road Trip Map paper. • Adhere one to each side of tag with glue stick. • Edge tag with Pinecone Ink.

ASSEMBLY:
Insert cards and envelopes into container. • Loop one end of ribbon through buckle and sew end of ribbon closed to prevent it from sliding off the buckle. Sew other end of the ribbon to make a clean edge that will not fray. • Thread other end of ribbon through buckle. Loop around card container and pull snugly. • Tie tag around the ribbon with string.

1. Fold and glue die cut.

2. Tear paper. Edge torn paper with ink.

3. Glue paper to box.

4. Decorate cards and envelopes.

12 Months of Tags
by Susan Keuter

January

MATERIALS: Holiday Sayings Sticker • Black Bottle Cap • 1 tag • Clock Face Sticker • Red grosgrain ribbon • Black fiber • Black Gingham paper • Eyelet • Date stamp • Ink: Black, Red • Eyelet tools • Mod Podge • Scrappy Glue

INSTRUCTIONS:
Cover the tag with Gingham paper. • Stamp the date on the clock sticker and adhere it to the tag with Mod Podge. • Edge the tag with Black ink. • Add the Red ribbon. Set the eyelet. Add the fiber. • Flatten the bottle cap. Add the sticker. • Glue the cap to the tag.

February

MATERIALS: Girl Pink Sayings Stickers • 1 tag • Cosmopolitan paper • "Cherish" Sticker • Heart eyelet • Date stamp • Rubber stamps: "hugs and kisses", "for you" • "laugh" Rub-On • Pink rickrack • Brown ribbon

INSTRUCTIONS:
Cover the tag with Cosmopolitan paper. • Stamp the date on the bottom. • Add the Pink rickrack. Set the eyelet. Add the fiber. • Print words under the word "Cherish".
• Add the stickers and rub-on. • Stamp the stickers with "hugs and kisses" and "for you".

March

MATERIALS: Papers: Target, Green Stripe • Gold Bottle Cap • 1 tag • Eyelet • Small Green Tag • Stencil Letter • AlphaBead Letters • Raffia • Ribbon • Gold Metallic Painters pen • 1" circle punch • *JudiKins* Diamond Glaze • Scrappy Glue

INSTRUCTIONS:
Cover the large tag with Green Stripe paper.
• Set an eyelet in the small tag. Add raffia through the eyelet. • Adhere the small Green tag, alphabeads, and stencil letter to the Green Stripe tag. • Punch a shamrock from the Target paper and glue it in the bottom of the cap. Let dry. • Fill the cap with Diamond Glaze. Let it set overnight.
• Ink the edges of the bottle cap with a Gold metallic painter, allowing some to run onto the Diamond Glaze.
• Adhere to tag with Scrappy Glue. Add ribbon.

April

MATERIALS: Silver Bottle Cap • 1 tag • Decorative paper • *"April"* Rub-On • White ribbon • Silver Metallic Painter pen • Hot Glue sticks in colors • Heat gun • Scrappy Glue

INSTRUCTIONS:
Fill a bottle cap with shaved pieces of the colored hot glue sticks. • Melt using a heat gun. Let cool. • Color the edges of the bottle cap with a Silver Metallic Painter. Let dry. • Cover the tag with Purple paper. • Cut out a flower from Plaid paper. • Adhere flower to the tag. • Glue the bottle cap to the flower. • Add rub-on and ribbon.

May

MATERIALS: Papers: School Books, Runaway Doll • Silver Bottle Cap • 1 tag • *KI Memories* paper • Ink: Brown, White • Metal Letters • Ribbon • Date stamp • Rub-On • Silver Metallic Painter pen • Hot Glue sticks in colors • Heat gun • Scrappy Glue

INSTRUCTIONS:
Flatten a bottle cap. • Fill the cap with shaved pieces of the metallic hot glue sticks. • Melt the hot glue with a heat gun. • While still warm, press the metal letters into the glue. Let the glue cool. • Color the edges of the bottle cap with a Silver Painter. • Cut out images and glue to tag. • Ink tag edges with Brown. • Add the ribbon. • Glue the bottle cap to the tag. • Stamp the date on the bottom of the tag in White.

June

MATERIALS: Fun and Games Stickers • 1 tag • *Bo Bunny Press* Denim Paper • Rub-On • Gold eyelet • *Memories in the Making* "june" sticker letters • 2 Watch Crystals • Beads • Photo saying • White shoelace • Adhesive

INSTRUCTIONS:
Line 2 watch crystals with adhesive. • Center beads on top of the bottle cap stickers and carefully place the watch crystal over the top.
• Cover a tag with denim paper. • Add rub-on, "june" sticker and photo saying.
• Adhere bottle cap stickers to the tag. • Set the eyelet. Thread the shoelace through the eyelet and tie a knot.

July

MATERIALS: Silver Bottle Cap • School Days Stickers • 1 tag • *The Paper Patch* paper • Date Rub-On • "USA" letters • Fibers • Ball chain • Square eyelet • Silver Metallic Painters pen • Embossing ink pad • Ultra Thick Embossing Enamel • Heat gun • Eyelet tools • Adhesive

INSTRUCTIONS:
Cover a tag with paper. Set the eyelet. • Add fibers and ball chain. Add letters and date and rub-ons. • Adhere a sticker to the bottle cap. • Tap the cap on an embossing pad and melt 2-3 layers of UTEE over the top. Let dry. • Color the edge of the bottle cap with a Silver Metallic Paint pen. • Glue bottle cap to the tag.

August

MATERIALS: Citrus Brights Stickers • 1 tag • *Print Works* Decorative paper • Stencil Letter • Rummage rubber stamps • Black ink • White Ultra Thick Embossing Enamel • Glue dots

INSTRUCTIONS:
Cover a tag with paper. • Cover the entire tag with stickers. • Randomly stamp words and dates onto stickers. • Cover a stencil letter with 2-3 layers of UTEE. • Adhere the stencil to the tag with glue dots.

September

MATERIALS: Gold Bottle Cap • 1 tag • Red cardstock • *Pixie Press* Decorative paper • Metal Letter • Gold Metallic Painter • Ribbon • Rummage rubber stamps • Red ink • 1" circle punch • *JudiKins* Diamond Glaze

INSTRUCTIONS:
Cover a tag with paper. • Stamp the alphabet in Red. Add a ribbon. • Flatten a bottle cap. • Punch a 1" circle of Red cardstock and glue it to the top of the cap. • Color a metal letter with a Gold Painter. • Adhere the letter to the cap with Diamond Glaze. Let dry. Fill in the letter with more Diamond Glaze. Let dry.

October

MATERIALS: 2 Black Bottle Caps • Holiday Sayings stickers • 1 tag • *NRN Designs* Decorative paper • Rub-On • Fibers • Mod Podge • Scrappy Glue

INSTRUCTIONS:
Flatten 2 bottle caps. • Apply stickers to caps and cover with a thick layer of Mod Podge. Let dry. • Cover the tag with Check paper. • Tear a strip of Black paper and adhere to the tag with Scrappy Glue. • Wrap fibers around tag. • Adhere the bottle caps to the tag. • Add ribbons.

November

MATERIALS: World Maps paper • Typewriter Alphabet Stickers • 1 tag • Metal Rimmed Tags • *me and my BIG ideas* stickers • Poetry Dog Tags • Metal Corners • Date Stamp • Black ink • Adhesive

INSTRUCTIONS:
Cover the tag with World Maps paper. • Stamp "November" in Black ink. • Add stickers, metal rimmed tag and metal corners. • Attach the dog tag with fibers.

December

MATERIALS: Christmas paper • Red Bottle Cap • 1 tag • Photo Flip • Brad • Date stamp • Red ink • *Dymo* Red Label tape • 1/8" hole punch

INSTRUCTIONS:
Cover a tag with Christmas paper. • Ink the edges of the tag and stamp the date with Red. • Print "Ho Ho Ho" with the *Dymo*. Adhere to the tag. • Add photo flip. • Flatten a bottle cap. Punch a 1/8" hole. • Fold cap over the edge on a counter top. Hammer again to tighten the fold line around the tag. • Add fibers.

It's About Time
by Mary Kaye Seckler

Do you have a collection of favorite quotes about time? If you need more, go to Google - "Time Quotes". This timely book is the perfect place to collect those thoughts.

MATERIALS: Vintage bottle cap paper • 3 sheets Kraft cardstock • 2" scrap Gold paper for clock hands • Stickers: Art Elements, Walnut Alphabet • Black bottle cap • 2 Black wire clips • 2⅜" metal disk • Tin • 1 Black brad • *Sizzix* Super Crescent Tag die cut • 9 Brown fibers • 4 clock charms • 4 brass ⅛" eyelets • 4 brass jump rings • 4 spiral paper clips • Rub-Ons: Small Providence, Small Heidi, Time definition • *Tsukineko* ink: Bark, Pinecone • Acrylic paint: Raw Umber, Cashmere Beige • Punches: Clock hands, Circles: 2", ¼" • Sponge brush • Bone folder • Drill • ⅛" drill bit • PVA glue • Glue stick • Glue dots

TIN INSTRUCTIONS:
Brush Cashmere Beige paint onto outside of tin base and disk. Let dry. • With brush nearly dry, add Raw Umber paint. • Drill a ⅛" hole in the center of the disk. Position disk on tin lid and mark the hole. Drill a hole in the tin lid. • Punch a 2" circle of Vintage paper. Adhere to disk with glue stick. • Punch clock hands from Gold paper. Glue to disk. • Insert a Black brad through center of decorated disk and tin lid. • Add 'Time' stickers below disk on tin lid. • Trace tin lid and base on Vintage paper. Cut out slightly smaller than markings. Adhere inside tin with PVA glue.

BOOK INSTRUCTIONS:
Print eight 'time' quotes on Kraft cardstock. • Die cut quotes plus 1 blank for cover. • Score each tag ⅜" from square end. • Edge all tags with Bark and Pinecone ink. • Set a brass eyelet in the bottom of four tags, staggered so that all charms can be seen when book is closed. • Attach charms with brass jump rings. • Add spiral paper clips to the other four tags, staggered across tops of tags. • Add fibers to tags.

Book cover: Tear out 'Time' definition and ink the edges. • Flatten a Black bottle cap. Apply clock sticker. • Create title with rub-ons. • Adhere Time definition in bottom left corner. • Adhere the clock bottle cap with a glue dot.

Book Assembly: Stack tags, alternating charm and paper clip tags, and fasten binder clips onto left side of book. Remove silver handles of clips.

1. Fold tag ⅜" from the edge.

2. Set eyelets.

3. Attach spiral paper clips.

4. Thread ribbons through holes and attach clips.

Unique

by Judy Ross

Next time you need something really special, make this card with a stained glass look.

MATERIALS: Papers: da Vinci Diamond, da Vinci Tiles • 2 sheets Black cardstock • Coffee Words stickers • Black metal clip • Black fiber • Micro beads • PeelnStick adhesive • Foam tape • Glue

INSTRUCTIONS:
Cut cardstock 6½" x 10". Fold to 5" x 6½". • Cut da Vinci Diamond paper 4¾" x 6". Glue to card. • Cut Black cardstock 4" x 5". Adhere to card with foam tape. Apply Coffee Words stickers. • Cut Black cardstock 3½" x 3½". • Cut 4 connecting images from da Vinci Tiles paper. • Glue Tiles to Black square. • Cover with PeelnStick. • Remove top adhesive film and cover with micro beads. • Attach Black clip. Adhere to card. • Tie with fibers.

CROWN PATTERN
FOR NUMBER 1 DAD TAG

Number 1 Dad Tag

by Judy Ross

Make Dad feel special with his own tag. Let it adorn a package or better yet, let it be his place card on his special day! The kids can help you make this tribute to Dad.

MATERIALS: da Vinci script paper • 3" square cardstock • Gold bottle cap • Stickers: da Vinci tags, Walnut Numbers • 2⅜" x 4⅞" shipping tag • 3 small Gold safety pins • Brown strip ribbon • Gold chain • Sepia ink pad • Crown pattern • Alphabet stamps • Glue

INSTRUCTIONS:
Trace crown onto cardstock. • Glue da Vinci paper on other side. • Cut out crown. • Ink tag and crown with Sepia. • Wrap ribbon around crown. • Pin tags onto ribbon. • Adhere crown to tag.• Flatten bottle cap. • Affix "1" sticker. Glue to tag. • Stamp "NO". • Add Gold chain.

Notes Clipboard

by Wendy Malichio

Tired of putting notes on the refrigerator door? Hang up this handy alternative with a clip and envelope to store your messages.

MATERIALS: Papers: da Vinci Script, da Vinci Tiles • 5½" x 9" Black cardstock • Silver Metal Clip • Silver Bottle Cap • Stickers: Typewriter Alphabet, Coffee Words • 5" x 8½" chipboard • 2 Silver brads • String • Coin envelope • Ribbon • *Ranger* ink • Glue

INSTRUCTIONS:
Cover chipboard with da Vinci Tiles paper. • Add Typewriter stickers and clip. • Ink the edges of the coin envelope. • Add brads to make the closure. Wrap string around the brads. • Tear a piece of Script paper. Ink the edges. Adhere to envelope. • Add stickers, bottle cap, and ribbon. Adhere envelope to board. • Attach ribbon to the back of the board for a hanger. • Mat with Black cardstock.

Family

by Judy Ross

Share vintage photos of your family with these great papers and embellishments.

MATERIALS: Papers: da Vinci Tiles, da Vinci Script • *Bazzill* cardstock: Tanner , Apricot, Black • Kraft mini-file folder • Coffee Words stickers • 2 Black Metal Clips • Printed twill • 3 Gold and Black buttons • 2 photos • Foam tape • Glue

INSTRUCTIONS:
Cut Tanner cardstock 7" x 10". Fold to 5" x 7".
• Cut Apricot cardstock 3⅞" x 5⅝". • Cut da Vinci tiles 3⅜" x 5⅛".
• Punch ¾" squares in bottom tiles. • Glue Black cardstock behind punched squares.
• Adhere tiles to card and glue buttons over Black squares. • Cover file folder with da Vinci script paper. • Put "family" sticker onto tab.
• Wrap folder with script twill. • Put clips on twill and hang 2 of the punched squares. • Put family photos in folder and mount to card with foam tape.

Buttons & Bows

by Judy Ross

Try collaging three patterns and then tie them all together with buttons and bows! You'll love the look.

MATERIALS: Papers: Linen Small Floral, da Vinci Script, da Vinci Brocade • Kraft cardstock • Coffee Words stickers • Silver metal clip • Small tag • 3 Peach buttons • *Ranger* Peeled Paint Distress ink • 18" Dashes ribbon • Dots & Checks ribbon • Stipple brush • Foam tape • Glue

INSTRUCTIONS:
Cut Kraft cardstock 5½" x 8½". Fold to 4¼" x 5½". • Cut Linen Small Floral paper 4¼" x 5½". Ink the edges. Adhere to card. • Tear da Vinci Script 2½" x 4¼". Ink the edges. Adhere to the left side of card. • Tear da Vinci Brocade papers to roughly cover the upper right corner. Ink the edges. Adhere to card. • Cut out a flower from the da Vinci Brocade paper and glue to card.
• Glue ribbon over the seam between the Script and Brocade papers. Adhere 5 bows.
• Stipple tag and word sticker. Adhere to card with foam tape. • Glue buttons in place. • Add clip and scrap papers.

My Beautiful Blessing

by Judy Ross

Add interest to your card by collaging different paper combinations together. Then add texture and dimension with buttons, ribbon, ball chains and stickers.

MATERIALS: Papers: da Vinci Brocade, da Vinci Script • Tan cardstock • Stickers: da Vinci Tags; Coffee Words • Beige grosgrain ribbon • 2 Gold ball chains • Buttons: 2 Peach,1 Tan • Foam tape • Glue

INSTRUCTIONS:
Cut Tan cardstock 5½" x 8½". Fold to 4¼" x 5½". • Tear da Vinci Script 2" x 2½". Adhere to card. • Cut da Vinci Brocade 3½" x 4¼". Tear the edge as shown in photo. Adhere to card. • Put 2 Gold chains onto tags. Mount to card with foam tape. • Wrap ribbon around card. • Apply word stickers onto ribbon. • Glue buttons in place.

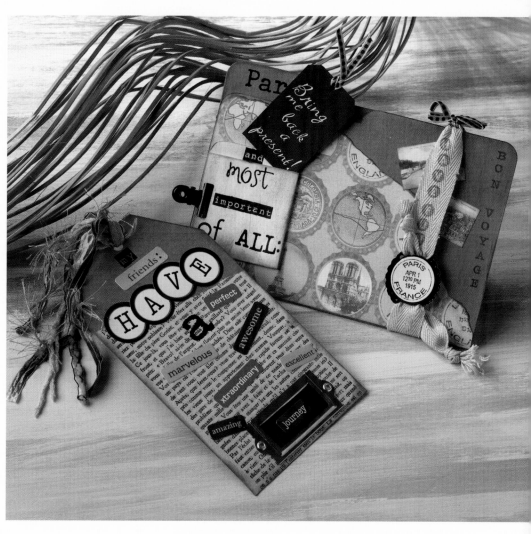

1. Flatten bottle cap.

2. Punch ¹/₁₆" holes to make a gap wide enough for the twill.

3. File the rough edges.

4. Thread twill through holes.

5. Apply sticker to cap.

Bon Voyage

by Mary Kaye Seckler

Next time you have a friend traveling to some distant adventure, wish them "Bon Voyage" with this eclectic travel card.

MATERIALS: Papers: Vintage, Road Trip Map • Black Bottle Cap • Black metal clip • Stickers: Typewriter Alphabet, Vintage Children, Coffee Words, Travel Milestones • French text • 5" x 7" File folder • 2¼" x 2½" library pocket • Ivory twill tape • Thin chipboard • Fibers: Brown, Rust • 1½" x 2½" Black tag • Brass label holder • 2 brass eyelets • Rub-ons: Small Heidi, small Destination, small Trademark, small and large Providence • 2 Vintage postcards • Black Label Maker, White Heber, Black Heber • Rubber stamps (*Just Rite* vertical title stamper; *Tin Can Mail* cancellation; *Treasure Cay* postmark; *PSX* Buttons alphabet set) • *Tsukineko* ink (Versamagic: Sahara Sand, Sierra Vista, Jumbo Java; Versacolor: Bark, Pinecone) • Jewelry file • ¹/₁₆" hole punch • Glue stick

INSTRUCTIONS:

File Folder: Edge the folder with 3 Versamagic pads and 2 Versacolor shades. • Stamp Bon Voyage in Java on right side of front flap of file. • Tear a piece of Vintage paper. Edge in Bark ink and glue to front of file. • Glue 2 small postcards in top right corner of file. • Tear Road Trip Map paper, wrinkle and flatten out, age with Bark ink and glue to back of file. Add sticker from Travel Milestones in top right corner. • Add 'Paris' with Trademark rub-ons.

Small Library Pocket: Age small library pocket with Versamagic colors. • Add 'most' using Heidi rub-ons. • Add 'important' with Label Maker rub-ons. • Add 'of' using Destination rub-ons and 'ALL' using Trademark rub-ons. • Add 'Bring me back a present' to Black tag using White Heber letters. • Add a ribbon to tag and insert tag in pocket. Clip pocket to front of file.

Tag: Cut tag 3¾" x 6¾" from thin chipboard. Edge in Bark ink. • Tear French text and age with Bark ink. Glue to front of tag. • Create greeting with rub-ons and stickers to say "my friends: Have a perfect, marvelous, awesome, xtraordinary, amazing, excellent journey". • Add brass label holder with brass eyelets. • Add collage ephemera to back of tag. • Stamp postmark and cancellation at random on back of tag. • Add fibers and insert tag into file.

File Tie: Flatten a bottle cap. Punch a row of ¹/₁₆" holes on each side of the cap. • File the rough edges smooth with a jewelry file. • Thread both ends of twill through the holes and knot ends. • Add "Paris" sticker to cap. • Stamp 'Have Fun' with Buttons stamps on twill in Java ink. • Tie a piece of ribbon at tip of tie. Add tie to file and pull ends to tighten.

da Vinci Mini Book

by Michele Charles

This is a great opportunity to play with collage and indulge in a variety of beautiful papers and embell-ishments.

MATERIALS: Papers: Da Vinci Script, da Vinci Tiles, da Vinci Diamond • 5 Brass Bottle Caps • Stickers: Coffee Words, da Vinci Tags, Art Elements • *Colorbox* Sepia Black pigment ink • 12" Ribbon • Foam Squares • Glue

INSTRUCTIONS:
Cut da Vinci Script paper into 4 strips of 3" x 12". • To create book signature, fold paper strip in half. • Open and fold outside ends to center crease. Glue flaps down. • Fold in half. • Do this to all 4 strips of paper. • Edge book signatures with Sepia Black pigment ink. • Rub or buff gently to blend ink into paper. • Collate signatures. Tie with ribbon. • Decorate book pages with stickers, bottle caps, da Vinci Tiles paper and da Vinci Diamonds paper. • Use foam squares to adhere bottle caps.

It's A Wild Journey

by Judy Ross

Beautifully coordinated colors give this card a fresh look.

MATERIALS: da Vinci Tiles paper • *Bazzill* cardstock: Apricot, Parakeet, Hillary • Coffee words stickers • 2 Black eyelets • Green and Pink Check ribbon • Eyelet tools • Foam tape • Glue

INSTRUCTIONS:
Cut Parakeet cardstock 7" x 9½". Fold to 4¾" x 7". • Cut Apricot cardstock 3½" x 6". Adhere to card with foam tape. • Cut Hillary cardstock 2¾" x 5". Set eyelets as in photo. • Insert ribbon in eyelets. Wrap around card. Glue 3 bows in place. • Cut 3 squares from da Vinci Tiles paper. Glue in place. • Apply word stickers.

Mini File Folders

by Michele Charles

When you are in the mood for a small project, these file folders are sure to please. Fun to make and simple to do, you can fill an hour with an artistic experience.

Journal

MATERIALS: Tim Holtz Rulers cardstock • Manila mini-file folder • Cutable strips: Light Words, Typewriter, Letter Squares • Adhesive • *Ranger* Vintage Photo Distress Ink • Red string

INSTRUCTIONS:
Cut out images, letters, and word from doo-dads. Ink as desired. • Adhere to folder. Wrap with string.

Wonder

MATERIALS: Tim Holtz Postale cardstock • Black mini file folder • Cutable strips: Typewriter, Light Words • Silver wire clip • *Ranger* Black Soot Distress Ink • Adhesive

INSTRUCTIONS:
Tear Postale cardstock. Ink as desired. Adhere to folder. • Add doo-dads and wire clip.

Life

MATERIALS: Tim Holtz Rulers cardstock • Kraft mini-file folder • Cutable strips: Letter Squares • *Ranger* Vintage Photo Distress Ink • Adhesive

INSTRUCTIONS:
Cut out ruler, letters, and word from doo-dads. Ink as desired. • Adhere to folder

Wishing You Happiness

by Judy Ross

Bottle cap stickers are wonderful for making medallions. Use chipboard as the base, add the stickers and embellish with crystals. Wow! You've got an elegant look with little effort.

MATERIALS: Linen Large Floral paper • Cardstock: Brown, Tan • Stickers: Coffee Words, Walnut Numbers • Chipboard • *Krylon* Copper leafing pen • *USArtQuest* mica • Rusty tin photo corner • 10" Brown Stripe ribbon • 4 clear rhinestone crystals • *JudiKins* Diamond Glaze • Glue

INSTRUCTIONS:
Cut Brown cardstock 8" square. Fold to 4" x 8". • Cut Tan cardstock 3" x 6" and edge with leafing pen. Glue in place. • Cut chipboard 2¼" x 5½". Cover with Linen Large Floral paper. Edge with leafing pen. • Adhere 2" x 3" mica and metal corner with Diamond Glaze. Wrap with ribbon. Apply sticker.
• Medallions: Take 4 medallion stickers and place on chipboard. Cut out and edge with Copper pen. • Place one medallion in the center of the flower. Adhere 3 medallions across the bottom of the card. • Glue crystals on medallions.

I Can't Say
by Mary Kaye Seckler

You are extra special, quirky, original, extraordinary, irresistible, wonderful. I would say more, but I ran out of room on the tag! Your eclectic best friend deserves a birthday wish as unique as he or she is. Have fun making this one.

MATERIALS: Papers: Lime A-Z Word Blocks, Lime A-Z • Cardstock (Lime Green, Aqua) • Lime Green mulberry paper • Stickers: Blue-Green Words, Text Messages • Aqua bottle cap • Metal flowers • Metal label holder • Jelly label • Small Providence Rub-ons • Small plastic flowers • Clear envelope • Ribbon: Green gingham, Blue with Lime dots • 1/8" eyelets: Blue, Green • 1/16" Blue eyelet • *Marvy* 2¼" square Giga punch • Envelope template • Bone folder • Craft glue • Glue dots • Glue stick

CARD INSTRUCTIONS:
Cut Lime cardstock 8½" square. Fold to 4¼" x 8½". • Punch a 2¼" square from the top front panel.

Inside Card: Cut A-Z paper 4¼" x 8½". Glue it inside the card. • Punch 1/8" holes and set metal and plastic flowers with eyelets within the square window area. • Flatten a bottle cap and affix a 'winky' sticker. • Affix the bottle cap over the flowers with a glue dot. • Cut Lime cardstock 1¼" x 3½". Affix the jelly greeting and adhere to lower part of inside panel with glue dots. • Add greeting to inside left panel using rub-ons.

Card front: Affix clear envelope to front panel of card with glue dots. • Cut a piece of Aqua cardstock 1⅞" x 3⅞". • Clip corners off one end and punch a ¼" hole in the same end.
• Attach Green ribbon to tag hole with a Lark's Head knot. • Affix word stickers to tag and slide tag into clear envelope. • Affix 'xxxooo' label to metal label holder with craft glue. • Mount 'You Are' sticker to Aqua cardstock and add above window. • Tie ribbon to one end of label holder with a single knot. • Wrap ribbon around card for measurement and tie another knot to secure label holder. Trim excess.

ENVELOPE INSTRUCTIONS:
Dissemble a #10 envelope to use as a template and place on the wrong side of Lime A-Z paper. Trace, score and cut out. • Lay template on Lime mulberry and trace the top half. Cut out and glue to inside of envelope. • Add word stickers to bottom front corner and back flap of envelope.

Cherish Card

Cherish the little things, for they usually are the big things. Wishing you a happy birthday!

MATERIALS: Lime A-Z Word Blocks paper • Navy cardstock • 1/8" eyelets (3 Lime, 2 Navy) • 5 pieces Lime and Navy ribbon • Wise Words White rub-on • Jelly Greeting • *Tsukineko* Apple Versacolor ink • Glue stick

INSTRUCTIONS:
Cut Navy cardstock 5" square. • Tear Lime A-Z Word Blocks paper at a diagonal and ink the edges with Apple. • Adhere to card with glue stick. • Punch five 1/8" holes in the bottom right corner of card. • Set 3 Lime eyelets and 2 Navy eyelets in the holes. • Thread ribbons through eyelets and attach with Lark's Head knots. • Apply rub-on to the top right corner of card. Affix jelly greeting below rub-on.

Square Envelope
by Mary Kaye Seckler

Here's an easy, fun-shaped envelope to make.

MATERIALS: Lime A-Z Word Blocks paper • Navy cardstock • 2 Blue bottle caps • 2 flower sequins • 2 brass eyelets • 12" ribbon • 1/8" hole punch • Small drill • glue stick

INSTRUCTIONS:
Trace template pattern onto wrong side of Lime A-Z Word Blocks paper. • Cut out and Xyron to cardstock. • Punch 1/8" holes in two flaps as indicated on pattern. Score cardstock and fold envelope. • Flatten 2 Blue bottle caps. • Drill a 1/8" hole in the center of each cap with a Dremel tool. • Punch a 1/8" hole at the end of ribbon. • On one flap, adhere cap and flower sequin with a long reach eyelet. • On the other flap, layer a flower sequin, cap, and ribbon at the back of the bottle cap before setting with a long reach eyelet. • Fold envelope closed and wrap the ribbon to close.

PATTERN FOR SQUARE ENVELOPE
Place on fold ➔

1. Trace pattern and cut it out.

2. Adhere to cardstock and cut out.

3. Score and fold.

4. Punch holes.

5. Set flattened cap with eyelet.

Flower Pot Card

by Mary Kaye Seckler

Wild Card and Envelope Templates make this fun-shaped card so simple to make. Enjoy making several in your favorite color combinations.

MATERIALS: Lime A-Z paper • Cardstock: Lime, Blue • Text Messages sticker • Lime bottle cap • *Wordsworth* Wild Card and Envelope templates • Fibers: Green, Blue • *Tsukineko* Fresh Green Versacolor ink • Flower punch • Bone folder • Needle • Glue dots • Foam tape • Glue stick

INSTRUCTIONS:
Trace envelope template onto Lime A-Z paper. • Mark score lines with bone folder. Cut out and fold. • Trace top of envelope template again to make a flap liner. • Cut out and glue to envelope. • Flatten bottle cap. Affix sticker face. • Punch 6 flowers from Blue cardstock. • Adhere petals to the back of the bottle cap with glue dots. Set aside. • Trace 2 cards from Lime cardstock and edge with Fresh Green ink. • Sew a 1½" line down the center of the card. Sew 2 leaves to the stem. • Cut flower pot from Lime A-Z paper and edge with Fresh Green ink. • Affix to base of stem with foam tape. • Affix bottle cap flower to top of stem with glue dots. • Stamp greeting on the reverse side of second card. • Glue second card back to back with first card to hide sewing thread. • Punch a ¼" hole at top of card. Add fibers.

1. Trace template and cut out.

2. Score and fold.

3. Trace top part again. Cut out and glue to flap.

4. Adhere punched flowers to flattened cap.

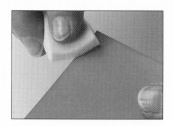

5. Cut 2 cards from template and edge with ink.

6. Stitch stem and leaves.

7. Cut out the flower pot. Ink the edges. Adhere to card with foam tape.

8. Glue stamped greeting to the back of the card.

Go Team Frame

by Janet Hopkins

Show off your all stars in a winning frame.

MATERIALS: Sports Pennants paper • Vintage Sports stickers • 3 Silver bottle caps • 8" x 8" Wood frame • Silver jump ring • Soccer Charm • *Ranger* Nick Bantock Van Dyke Brown ink • Brayer • PVA glue

INSTRUCTIONS:
Cut and adhere paper to the front of the frame with PVA glue. • Use a brayer to smooth out any wrinkles or bumps in the paper. Let dry. • Ink the edges of the frame. • Flatten 3 bottle caps. Apply a sticker in each one. • Punch a hole in the soccer ball bottle cap. Attach a jump ring and soccer charm. • Glue bottle caps in place.

Congrats

by Wendy Malichio

Choose cardstock in school colors for a unique graduation card.

MATERIALS: Papers: Sports Letters, Sports Pennants • *Bazzill* Cornucopia cardstock • Stickers: da Vinci ABC Tags, Road Trip ABC Tags • Ribbon • Rub-ons • Sandpaper

INSTRUCTIONS:
Cut Cornucopia cardstock 7¾" x 12". Fold to 6" x 7¾". • Cut Sports Pennants paper 4½" x 6¾". Cut Sports Letters paper 2½" x 7¼". • Sand the edges lightly to create a "White" border. Adhere papers to card. • Add stickers, ribbon and rub-ons to create a title.

Play Hard

by Janet Hopkins

Decorate dangling bottle caps with stickers to suit any sport.

MATERIALS: Sports Pennants paper • *Bazzill* Red cardstock • Bottle caps: Silver, Orange • Vintage Sports stickers • Metal clasp • Wonderful Words "Play Hard" Rub-ons • Ribbon • *Ranger* Nick Bantock Van Dyke Brown ink • Hole punch

INSTRUCTIONS:
Cut Red cardstock 5¼" x 8½". Fold to 4¼" x 5¼". • Cut Sports Pennant paper 4" x 5". • Ink the edges of the paper and stickers. • Flatten 2 bottle caps. Apply stickers inside. • Punch 2 small holes in the top of each bottle cap. Attach clasp. • Tie clasp to ribbon. Tape ribbon ends to the back of the Sports Pennants paper. • Adhere Sports Pennants paper to card front. • Apply rub-on words.

3 Cheers

by Wendy Malichio

"G" is for graduate. Cheer your graduate on to his or her next success with this unique card.

MATERIALS: Papers: Sports Letters, Sports Pennants • *Bazzill* cardstock: Bottle Glass, Dark Sand • Ribbon • Computer Fonts • Foam squares

INSTRUCTIONS:
Cut Bottle Glass cardstock 7" x 11½". Fold to 5¾" x 7". • Cut Pennant paper 4¾" x 5". Adhere to card. • Cut out the "G" from Sports Letters paper. Adhere to card. • Cut out a "flag" from the Sports Pennant. Adhere ribbons. Adhere to card with foam squares. • Computer print "3 Cheers for the Graduate" on Dark Sand cardstock. Adhere to card.

1. Die cut pocket and Ink the edges of the pocket.

2. Decorate with bottle caps.

3. Attach the closure with eyelets.

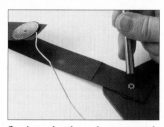

4. Punch a Black hole reinforcement.

5. Die cut card and ink the edge of the card.

6. Decorate with flattened bottle cap and sticker.

Our Champion

by Jane Hopkins

Say "thanks" to the coach with a card the entire team can sign. What a way to acknowledge a champion!

MATERIALS: Sports Letters paper • Red card • White insert • Grey "thanks" jelly sticker • "oach" Rub-ons • "Champion" Wonderful Words Rub-ons • *Ranger* Nick Bantock Van Dyke Brown ink • Metal letters (o, u, r) • Craft knife

INSTRUCTIONS:
Cut Sports Letters paper to cover the front of the card, keeping in mind the position of the "C" for coach. Cut out the window with a craft knife. • Distress the edges of the paper with ink. Adhere to the front of the card. • Adhere rub-ons. • Affix the metal letters for the word "our".
• Using the window as a guide, adhere the "thanks" jelly sticker in place.

Play Ball!

by Mary Kaye Seckler

This birthday coupon will be a sure winner with your favorite sports fan. This one is good for two tickets to opening day. Personalize yours for a perfect gift.

MATERIALS: Road trip Map paper • Cardstock: 1 Black, 2 Kraft • Bottle Caps: Blue, Red • Vintage Sports stickers • 2 long reach brass eyelets • Beige cord • Blue ribbon • Red ribbon • *Tsukineko* Pinecone ink • Hole punches (1", ⅝", ¼", ⅛") • *Accu-Cut* dies: Slash pocket, Scallop edge tag • Glue stick • Glue dots

POCKET INSTRUCTIONS:
Die-cut pocket from Kraft cardstock. • Fold pocket along score lines, seal pocket with glue stick and edge card and pocket with Pinecone ink. • Mount 2 baseball stickers on Black cardstock and punch out with 1" hole punch. • Punch a ⅛" hole in the center of each baseball. Set aside. • Cut a strip of Black cardstock 1¼" x 8¼". • Wrap around pocket with opening centered in front. • On the right side of the Black strip, set a baseball with a brass eyelet. • On the left side, do the same, adding the Beige cord in a loop between the baseball and the strip. • The eyelet will catch the cord. Wrap the cord around both baseballs to secure. • Trim the word 'New York' from the scrapbook paper and affix above the strip with glue stick. • Flatten a Blue bottle cap. Apply "Let's Play" sticker to cap. Adhere cap to pocket with a glue dot.

CARD INSTRUCTIONS:
Computer print coupon info and copy onto Kraft cardstock. • Die-cut tag and edge with Pinecone ink. • Hole reinforcement: Punch a ¼" hole in a scrap of Black cardstock. Punch a ⅝" hole centered around the first hole. Adhere reinforcement to top of tag with glue stick and punch hole in tag. • Add Red and Blue ribbons to tag. Flatten Red bottle cap and apply "Play Ball" sticker. • Affix bottle cap to tag with glue dot. Insert tag into pocket.

Father's Day
by Sherelle Christensen

Remind Dad of just how much he is appreciated by making a thoughtful card for him.

MATERIALS: Papers: Linen Houndstooth, Linen Stripe • Black cardstock • 3" Metal Disk • Black White Words stickers • Black pen • Colored pencils • E6000 adhesive • Glue stick

INSTRUCTIONS:
Cut Black cardstock 6¼" x 9½". Fold to 4¾" x 6¼". • Cut Linen Houndstooth paper 4½" x 6. Adhere to card. • Apply stickers to the edge. • Cut a White 2½" circle from Linen Stripe paper. Adhere inside the disk. • Write the title and make dots around the edge of the paper. Adhere disk to card with E6000.

Thanks
by Sherelle Christensen

Send a thank you card that will be remembered. This delightful collage has dimension, texture and sparkle.

MATERIALS: Linen Small Floral paper • Gray cardstock • Linen ABC Tags stickers • 3 clear rhinestone crystals • ⅛" wide ribbon: Black, White, Gray • 1½" x 8¼" White chenille fabric • Black pen • *Ranger* Distress Black Soot ink • Staples • E6000 adhesive • Glue stick

INSTRUCTIONS:
Cut Gray cardstock and Linen Small Floral 6¾" x 8¼". Adhere Linen paper to cardstock. Fold to 4⅛" x 6¾". Ink the card edges. • Staple White fabric across the outside of the card. • Adhere rhinestones with E6000. • Tie ribbons through Linen ABC Tags. Apply stickers to fabric on card front. • Write "thanks for your kindness" under the fabric across the card.

Wedding Day
by Sherelle Christensen

Celebrate that most special of occasions with a Black and White wedding card.

MATERIALS: Papers: Linen Vine, Linen Stripe • Black cardstock • Black metal clip • 24 clear rhinestone crystals • 3½" wide Black lace • Black pen • *Ranger* Distress Black Soot ink • E6000 adhesive • Foam squares • Glue stick

INSTRUCTIONS:
Cut Black cardstock 5¾" x 9½". Fold to 4¾" x 5¾". • Cut 2 pieces of Linen Vine paper 4⅜" x 5½". Ink the edges. Adhere one piece to the back of the card. Wrap lace around the center of the other piece. Adhere to the front of the card. • Adhere rhinestones to front of card with E6000. • From Linen Stripe paper, cut a Black 2½" square and a White 2¼" square. • Adhere the White paper to the Black mat. • Write "a little something for your Wedding Day". • Add the clip to the matted title and adhere to card with foam squares.

Our Wedding Day Frame

by Sherelle Christensen

Everyone has photos of someone's wedding. Display those cherished memories in this special frame.

MATERIALS: Papers: Linen Stripe, Linen Small Floral • Photo frame • 8 clear rhinestone crystals • Black ribbon • Colored pencils • Black pen • Mod Podge • Glue stick

INSTRUCTIONS:
Cut Linen Small Floral paper to fit frame. Adhere with Mod Podge. • Adhere rhinestones and ribbon. • From Linen Stripe paper, cut a Black 1½" x 5¾" strip and a White 1¼" x 5½" strip. • Adhere White strip to the Black mat. Write the title. Adhere to frame.

A Birthday Wish

by Judy Ross

Flat marbles add the touch of elegance to Black and White. Let them be the dimensional accent to your sticker message.

MATERIALS: Papers: Linen Diamond, Linen Small Floral, Linen Houndstooth • Black cardstock • Medium Black mini-file folder • Stickers: Typewriter alphabet, Black White Words, Vintage Faces • Silver Wire Clip • 15" Polka Dot ⅜" ribbon • 2 tickets • 8 clear ¾" flat marbles • JudiKins Diamond Glaze • Glue

INSTRUCTIONS:
Cut cardstock 7" x 10". Fold to 5" x 7". • Collage Linen Diamond and Linen Houndstooth papers onto card front. • Glue 7" of polka dot ribbon across card. • Cover folder with Linen Small Floral paper. Adhere "joy" sticker to tab. • Apply word stickers on folder. Wrap with ribbon. Adhere face sticker. • Stagger letter stickers onto card. Adhere marbles to letters with Diamond Glaze. • Glue folder onto card. Stuff with tickets. Attach clip onto ticket.

An Amazing Woman

by Judy Ross

Honor that awesome woman in your life with this remarkable card.

MATERIALS: Papers: Linen Small Floral, Linen Diamond • Black cardstock • 3 Black Bottle Caps • Stickers: Art Elements, Black-White Words • 3 clear watch crystals • 6 clear octagon 7 mm beads • 14" Black and White ribbon • JudiKins Diamond Glaze • Fabri-Tac adhesive • Glue stick

INSTRUCTIONS:
Cut cardstock 5½" x 8½". Fold to 4¼" x 5½". • Cut Linen Small Floral 2" x 5½", Linen Diamond 2¼" x 5½". Glue to card. • Adhere 5½" of ribbon over the seam where the papers meet with Fabri-Tac.• Apply stickers to bottle caps and adhere watch crystals over caps with Diamond Glaze. Glue to card. • Place word stickers on card and glue beads in place. • Make bow and adhere to card with Fabri-Tac.

Flower Card

by Karen Wells

Romantic flowers adorn a card that celebrates a wedding.

MATERIALS: Papers: Romance License, Romance Celebration • 5" x 11" Light Green cardstock • Metal Disk • Lace ribbon • Blossom flowers • Brads • *AccuCut* 4 pane window die-cut • Beige acrylic paint • Glue
TIP: If die-cut is unavailable, square punch can be used.

INSTRUCTIONS:
Fold cardstock to 5" x 5½". • Cut Romance License and Romance Celebration papers with die-cut. • Move cut squares to fit the window panes. • Glue to cardstock. • Adhere lace ribbon to the front of the card. • Paint the metal disk Beige. Let dry. • Cut out the seal from the License paper and adhere to disk. • Attach colored brads to blossom flowers and glue to disk. • Glue disk to card.

Marriage Blessing

by Karen Wells

May you share the blessing of a long and happy life together.

MATERIALS: Papers: Romance Hands, Romance License • 6¼" x 9" Cream cardstock • Black Coffee Words Sticker • Framed metal letter • Copper brad • Flower blossoms • Colored brads • Hole punches • Paper Shapers 1⅜" square punch

INSTRUCTIONS:
Fold cardstock to 4½" x 6¼". • Punch out square on card front. • Cut out the hands from Romance Hands paper and glue inside the card behind the square window. • Cut out borders from Romance Hands paper and fit to border the window. • Cut out word "Marriage" from the Romance License paper and glue to front of card. • Punch holes for flowers and attach blossoms to front of card with brads. • Punch hole for framed letter "A" and attach with Copper brad. • Place "blessing" sticker below the word "marriage".

Celebrate

by Karen Wells

Send your best wishes in a card.

MATERIALS: Romance License Paper • Cardstock: 7" x 10" White, 4" x 4¾" Grey • "Celebrate" metal word • Wired ribbon • *Ten Seconds Studio* (Aluminum metal, mold #8, tools: C29, paper stump) • Spackle • Acrylic paint (Goose Feather, Territorial Beige) • Nostalgia Edgers • The Ultimate! glue

INSTRUCTIONS:
Cut Romance License paper 3¾" x 4½". Adhere to Grey cardstock. • Cut out oval picture of bride and groom. • Cut 2¾" x 4" piece of metal. • Place oval in center of metal and using the ball and cup tool (C29), emboss around the oval. • Place metal on patterned mold and using the paper stump, rub pattern around the oval. • Apply spackle to back of raised surfaces of metal and let dry. • Paint the metal with Goose Feather acrylic paint and brush with Territorial Beige paint. Let dry. • Cut corners with edger scissors. • Glue oval to metal and adhere to Romance License paper. • Attach to White cardstock. • Cut ribbon to fit card and attach. Adhere "Celebrate" metal word to ribbon.

Love Flower Card

by Janet Hopkins

My love will bloom more beautifully than the rose and never fade. Make a romantic card to express your innermost feelings.

MATERIALS: Off White Match Book Card • *Bazzill* Green cardstock • Spring Flowers Postcards sticker • Jump ring • Love rub-ons • Eyelets • Ribbon • Small jeweler's tag • *Ranger* Nick Bantock Van Dyke Brown ink • Sandpaper

INSTRUCTIONS:
Cut Green cardstock 2¾" x 3⅞". Apply flower sticker. Distress the edges with sandpaper and ink. • Tie ribbon and knot in the front. Tape the ribbon ends to the back of the mat. • Apply "love" rub-on to tag. Attach jump ring to tag and through the knot in the ribbon. • Adhere the entire piece to the front of the card. • Embellish the envelope with ribbon as well for a finishing touch.

Remember CD Case

by Karen Wells

Remember your special day with photos on a CD stored lovingly in a gorgeous case made just for this occasion.

MATERIALS: CD holder • Papers: Romance Celebration, Romance Hands • Stickers: Vintage Faces, Spring Flowers Postcards • White Bottle Cap • Tan word ribbon • Ribbon: Lace, Wine, Green • Beige acrylic paint • Glue

INSTRUCTIONS:
Cut Romance Hands paper to fit front of CD holder. • Cut out the 'hands' and glue to front of the cover. • Glue the Green and Tan worded ribbons to border the top and bottom of holder. • Cut Romance Celebration paper to fit the inside of CD holder and glue in place. • Cut paper to fit the holder and line with Green ribbon. • Affix the "A Joyous Day" sticker. • Cut Wine and lace ribbon to cover the edges of the CD cover and glue down, folding over the edges. • Paint the bottle cap Beige. Let dry. Affix the rose sticker inside and glue to cover. • Place photo CD inside.

Happy Halloween

by Sally Traidman

Here's a creative way to use your small stamps to turn a plain White card into something visually interesting. The bottle cap accent adds dimension to the card.

MATERIALS: White cardstock • Black Bottle Cap • Holiday Sayings stickers • Check ribbon • Rubber stamps (*Mostly Hearts:* Halloween minis, small circle; *Hero Arts* Circle) • Ink: Orange, Yellow, Gold, Black • Foam tape

INSTRUCTIONS:

Card: Cut White cardstock 6" x 8½". Fold to 4¼" x 6". • Stamp the Hero Arts circle in Orange, Yellow and Gold to fill the card. • Ink smaller circle on top of some areas. • Stamp several Halloween images in Black.

Accents: Flatten a Black bottle cap. Apply sticker. • Cut 4" of ribbon. Fold the ribbon in half. • Adhere the ribbon to the back of the bottle cap. • Adhere the cap to the card with foam tape.

Boo!

by Susan Keuter

Boo! Make a great card accent with an orange bottle cap and sticker.

MATERIALS: *Bazzill* cardstock: Black, White • *NRN Designs* Decorative Paper • Orange Bottle Cap • Holiday Sayings stickers • Rub-On • Black fiber • Edge Clips • ⅛" hole punch • *JudiKins* Diamond Glaze

INSTRUCTIONS:

Cut Black cardstock 6" x 12". Fold in half to 6" x 6". • Cut a White mat 5½" x 5½". Cut a Check mat 5¼" x 5¼". • Flatten a bottle cap. • Punch 2 holes opposite each other on the edge of the bottle cap. • Adhere sticker. • Cover the sticker and cap with Diamond Glaze. Let dry overnight. • Thread fiber through the holes in the bottle cap and clip to the edges of your mats. • Glue mats to the card. • Add "Boo" Rub-On.

Felt Spider

This itsy bitsy spider adds that perfect touch to any Halloween decoration.

MATERIALS: Fine Black wire • 3 foam dots • Black felt (½" circle, body shape) • 2 Red seed beads • E6000 adhesive

INSTRUCTIONS:

Cut out the body shape using the pattern. • Cut 4 pieces of wire 2" long. • Lay the wires evenly across a foam dot. • Place another foam dot over the wires. • Cover the foam dot with the felt body. • Add another foam dot. Add the felt circle. • Glue the seed beads to the head. • Carefully shape the legs. • Adhere the bottom foam dot to the card.

FELT SPIDER
PATTERN

Boo Ghosts!

by Sally Traidman

Casper the friendly ghost and friends will be inviting your guests to a scary party, or just wishing them a ghostly Halloween. Add google eyes to the ghosts for more fun!

MATERIALS: Cardstock: Orange, Black, White • Orange Bottle Cap • Holiday Sayings sticker • Halloween ribbon • *Hero Arts* Ghost stamp • Black ink • Nail • Hammer • Sewing machine • Orange thread • Old sewing machine needle • Mounting tape

INSTRUCTIONS:
Card: Cut Orange cardstock 5½" x 8½". Fold to 4¼" x 5½". • Cut an odd-sized Black scrap and stitch it to the card. • Sew around the edge of the front of the card.
Accents: Flatten 1 Orange bottle cap. • Punch a hole and affix the Halloween ribbon. • Apply a Boo sticker. Adhere cap to the card with mounting tape. • Ink the ghost stamp with Black, but do not ink "boo" area. • Stamp onto White cardstock. • Cut out ghosts and adhere to the card.

Trick or Treat

by Sally Traidman

This card is a real treat to make - no tricks involved! With a sewing machine, you can make this card in less than 10 minutes. Just be sure to use an old needle in your machine. I save my old needles for sewing on paper.

MATERIALS: Cardstock: Gold check, Orange, Black • Orange Bottle Cap • Holiday Sayings sticker • Trick or Treat ribbon • Sewing machine • Orange thread • Old sewing machine needle • Double-sided tape • Foam tape

INSTRUCTIONS:
Card: Cut Gold check cardstock 5½" x 7". • Fold to 2¾" x 7". • Cut an Orange mat 1¼" x 6". • Cut a Black mat 1" x 5¾". • Stitch mats together. Tape mats to the card. • Cut Trick or Treat ribbon 5¼" long. Tape the ribbon to the card.
Accent: Flatten 1 Orange bottle cap and apply the sticker. • Adhere cap with foam tape.

Halloween

by Sally Traidman

If you love to play with window cards, this Halloween card won't scare you at all. The beige paper complements the orange, creating a festive fall greeting.

MATERIALS: Cardstock: Orange, White • Beige paper • Black Bottle Cap • Holiday Sayings sticker • Ribbon • 2 Gold mini brads • Tiny White envelope • *Hero Arts* Happy Halloween stamp • Sand ink • Craft knife • Glue

INSTRUCTIONS:
Cut White cardstock 5¼" x 10½". Fold to 5¼" square. • Cut a 2¾" window in the middle of the card front. • Wrap the card front with Orange cardstock. • Stamp "Happy Halloween" on a 3" square of Beige paper with Sand ink. • Glue the Beige paper to the inside of the window so the words show through the window. • Cut a tiny Orange note card to fit in the tiny White envelope. Glue envelope in place. • Flatten 1 Black bottle cap and affix a sticker. Tuck the bottle cap into the envelope and glue in place. • Cut ribbon 2½" long and attach it to the card with Gold mini brads. • Cover the inside of the card front with White cardstock.

Lantern Card

by Judy Claxton

Use coordinating colors in multiple layers to give emphasis to the central image on your project.

MATERIALS: Halloween Collage paper • Cardstock: Black, Goldenrod Gray • Piece of Joss paper with Gold center • Decorative papers • Orange Bottle Cap • Holiday Sayings stickers • 4 photo corners • Fine line Black permanent marker • *Tsukineko* StazOn Black ink • Rubber stamps (*Coronado Island Bloomers*; *Magenta* small round sunburst) • E6000 adhesive • Double-stick tape

INSTRUCTIONS:
Card: Cut Black cardstock 6¼" x 8½". Fold to 4¼" x 6¼". Cut joss paper to size. Glue the joss paper to the Black. • Tear the Goldenrod cardstock around the edges and stamp with both images in Black ink. Attach to card at an angle. • Layer other papers onto the card as desired. • Cut out the image of the boy with a Jack-O-Lantern. Cut a Gray mat ¼" larger than the image. Adhere the image to the mat with Gold photo corners. Tape the mat in place.
Accent: Flatten the bottle cap. Attach a sticker to the cap. Draw dots and edge the cap with a Black marker. • Attach the cap to the card with E6000.
• Draw dots on joss paper with a Black marker.

Halloween Fold-Out

MATERIALS: Papers: Halloween Collage, Pumpkins, Trick or Treat • Cardstock: Textured, Orange • Orange Bottle Cap • Holiday Sayings stickers • Orange/White ¼" wide ribbon • *Jolee's Boutique* Spider • 6 google eyes • Corner Rounder punch • Ink: *Tsukineko* StazOn Black; *Ranger* Distress Antique Linen • Sponge • *Xyron* adhesive • E6000 adhesive • Velcro scrap • Glue stick

INSTRUCTIONS:
Card: Cut a strip 4" x 9½" from Textured and Trick or Treat papers. Glue papers together. • Following diagram, fold and trim card edge. • Lightly sponge Trick or Treat paper with Antique Linen ink. **Inside:** Cut an Orange 3¼" square and round the corners. Glue it in place. • Cut the Pumpkin paper 3" x 3¼". Glue it over the Orange square.
• Cut out the "trick or treat" words from Trick or Treat paper. Glue it diagonally onto the bottom section of the card. Add 2 stickers. • **Inside booklet:** Cut a strip of Textured paper 2½" x 5". Fold it in half and round the corners. • Lightly sponge the inside of the booklet with Antique Linen ink and smudge with a Black ink. • Cut out the image of the witch from the Halloween Collage paper. Round the corners. Cut an Orange square ¼" larger than the witch and round the corners. Glue the Witch to the Orange and glue it to the booklet. Add the spider web and bottle cap sticker. to the top inside flap. **Booklet cover:** Glue the ribbon in place. • Cut out 2 pumpkins from Pumpkins paper and glue in place. Add google eyes. • Flatten a bottle cap and add a sticker. Adhere the cap to the booklet with E6000. Adhere the booklet over the Pumpkin/ Orange square. • **Outside:** Cut out a large pumpkin from Pumpkins paper. Lightly sponge it with Antique Linen ink. Adhere google eyes with E6000. Glue the pumpkin to the point of the flap. Glue the ribbon in place. Tear "Magic Halloween" from the Halloween Collage paper and glue it and the spider to the card. • **Closure:** Cut a small square of Velcro. Keep both pieces together. Attach one part to the underside of the pumpkin. Fold the card closed. Glue the other part of the Velcro in place.

Halloween Fold-Out

by Judy Claxton

This creative card keeps opening, and opening. Inside, there is a flap. Lift it to reveal another set of spooky images. Be sure you check out the techniques for using mounts. The closure on this card is a scrap of velcro - very clever!

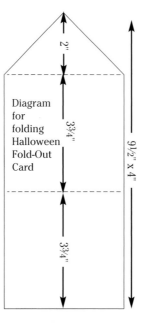

Diagram for folding Halloween Fold-Out Card

2"

3¾"

3¾"

9½" x 4"

Halloween Clock

by Judy Claxton

Make every hour the 'witching hour' with this creative Halloween clock.

MATERIALS: Papers: Trick or Treat, Halloween Collage • Cardstock • 4 Black Bottle Caps • Holiday Sayings stickers • *PSX* Fall Leaves paper • Clock works • 45 Record • Die cuts: Witch, Moon • ¼" wide Black stitched ribbon • *Ranger*: Glossy Accents; Antique Linen Distress Ink • Google eyes: 4 large, 2 small • Copic Air Brush • Orange marker • Mod Podge • Polyurethane Gloss Varnish • 1" circle punch • E6000 adhesive

INSTRUCTIONS:

Clock: Airbrush all the pumpkins and the moon with an Orange marker. • Use Mod Podge to collage the front of the record with papers, cut-outs from the Fall Leaves paper, pumpkins from the Halloween Collage paper, laser cuts, Black ribbon, and the "trick or treat" words cut from Trick or Treat paper.

• Cover the back of the record with Trick or Treat paper. • Use Glossy Accents on the eyes of the pumpkins to give dimension. Let dry. • Brush on 2 coats of varnish. Let dry. • Adhere the google eyes to the pumpkins with E6000. • Install the clock work through the center of the record.

Bottle caps: Cut out a small pumpkin with the circle punch. • Spray with Orange marker using the airbrush.

• Attach the pumpkin to a Black bottle cap. • Attach the Halloween stickers to the remaining bottle caps. • Attach caps to the clock with E6000.

Spooky Spider

by Janie Ray

Create a clever spider to creep along the table or to hang on an invisible string

MATERIALS: Black Bottle Cap • Holiday Sayings stickers • 20 gauge Black wire • 2 small Black cardstock circles • 2 tiny Orange rhinestones • E6000 adhesive • Glue

INSTRUCTIONS:

Flatten a bottle cap. Punch 4 holes in each side of the bottle cap.

• Cut 4 pieces of wire, each 8" long. • Insert a wire through each hole on one side of the cap. • Twist all 4 wires together under the cap for about ½". • Insert wires through each hole on the other side of the cap. • Curl the ends of the wire to form 'feet'. • Add a sticker to the top of the spider. • Glue rhinestones to circles and glue in place.

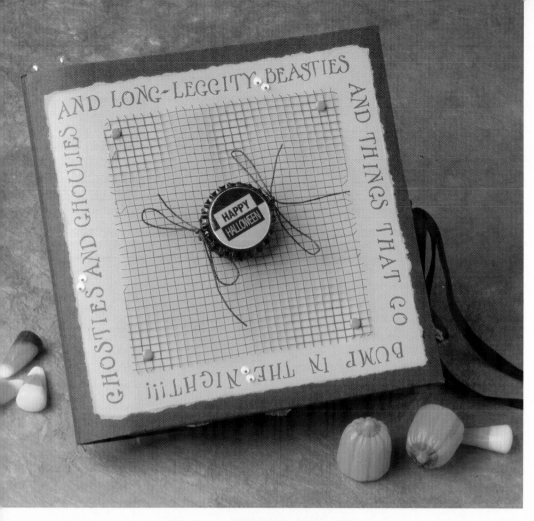

Halloween Booklet Cover

by Mary Kaye Seckler

Scare up your collection of Halloween photos and make this bewitching scrapbook. The cover features a "boo"tiful spider hiding a secret message in an accordion fold container.

MATERIALS: Cardstock: 6" square Lime Green, 1" x 12" Orange • 2 Black Bottle Caps • Holiday Sayings stickers • Metal mesh 4" square • 1" x 12" blank newsprint • 4 pieces of 6" Black waxed linen thread • *Making Memories:* Black Mini Book, 4 Orange mini brads, Chunky Black letter stickers • 6 mini google eyes • *Hero Arts* Playful rubber stamp alphabet 5 • *Tsukineko* ink (Black Brilliance, Green Versacolor, Paper Shapers 1" hole punch) • *McGill* 1/16" hole punch • Ruler

INSTRUCTIONS:
Cardstock: Tear Lime cardstock using a ruler. • Edge with Green ink. • Stamp the title in Black ink around the card perimeter. • Crumple metal mesh and attach to Lime cardstock with brads. • Adhere card to cover with PVA glue. • Adhere google eyes with PVA glue.

Bottle Cap Spider: Fold blank newsprint in an accordion that is a bit less than 1" wide. • Punch with 1" hole punch to form a round accordion piece template. • Trace this template onto Orange cardstock. (Orange cardstock is too thick to punch an accordion directly.) • Cut out the accordion and score lines between the circles where the accordion will fold. • Attach bottle cap stickers and 'Spooky' stickers.
• Punch 1/16" holes on each side of both bottle caps for closure.
• Attach Black waxed linen thread through holes. (The thread ends will be hidden under the accordion.)
• Apply PVA glue to the inside of the bottle caps and adhere the accordion ends to the caps. • Put caps together and tie closed. • Arrange closure threads to resemble spider's legs. • Adhere bottle cap spider to the center of the front cover with a glue dot.

Inside Pages: Refer to photos and embellish as desired.

Make a Bottle Cap Shaker

1. Apply sticker and fill cap with shaker pieces. Apply glue to edge.

2. Place acetate over cap. Let dry.

3. Trim away excess acetate.

How to Make Bottle Cap Jelly Beans

1. Melt UTEE in a melting pot.

2. Fill a slightly bent bottle cap with UTEE. Let cool.

3. Color cooled UTEE with a marker.

Make a Bottle Cap Accordion Fold-out.

1. Accordion fold strip of newsprint. Punch.

2. Trace the newsprint template.

3. Cut out, score, and fold the accordion.

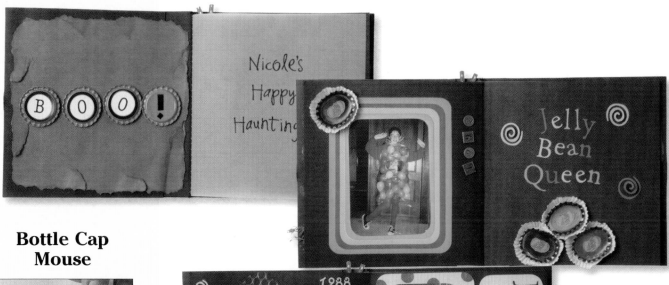

Bottle Cap Mouse

1. Punch 2 circles for mouse ears.

2. Ink the ear edges.

3. Stain the cap edge with alcohol ink. Let dry.

4. Glue whiskers in place.

5. Apply sticker over wires. Adhere ears to the back of the cap.

Snowman Card

by Molly Jennings

Frosty will cheerfully bring holiday greetings to your friends, but he would also make a fun birthday greeting or "thinking of you".

MATERIALS: Cardstock: White, Black • Blue Dotted paper • Gold Bottle Cap • *Hero Arts* tiny buttons: Red, Green • Two 4" lengths Red eyelash yarn • Acrylic paint: White, Orange, Black, Pink • Clear enamel spray • Glue • Foam dots

INSTRUCTIONS:

Bottle cap: Flatten the bottle cap. • Paint cap with several coats of White. Let dry. • Paint the face. Let dry. Spray lightly with enamel.

Card: Cut White cardstock 5½" x 8½". • Fold card to 4¼" x 5½". • Cut the Blue Dotted paper 2½" x 2¾" and glue it to the card.

Accents: Cut out a Black hat. • Glue the bottle cap to the card. Glue the hat in place. • Add foam dots under the top section of the hat. • Tie both pieces of yarn together with an Overhand Knot close to one end. • Glue the fibers and buttons in place.

HAT
PATTERN

Holly Gift Card

by Lynn Krucke

Beautiful gift wrappings don't have to be difficult or expensive. Make the gift giving experience memorable with these quick embellishments. Make a gift even more special with a handmade tag. These ideas will get your creativity flowing!

LEAF
PATTERN

MATERIALS:
Christmas paper
• 2 shades of Green cardstock
• 3 Red Bottle Caps
• Gift box • Ribbon
• E6000 glue

INSTRUCTIONS:
Wrap a small gift box with Christmas paper. • Tie ribbon near one end. • Cut 2 holly leaves from Green cardstock.
• Crease along the center and use your fingers to gently shape the leaves.
• Flatten bottle caps.
• Adhere holly leaves and caps to the box.

Joy

MATERIALS: Christmas paper • Gold star • Gold wire • Jingle bell • Dark Green gel pen

INSTRUCTIONS:
Apply Gold foil to tag edges and top of cap • Make Green dots around the circle on the paper to enhance the design. • Add the Gold star. • Punch a hole in the edge of cap. • Wire a jingle bell to the cap. • Cut the word "joy" from Christmas paper, adhere to the cap.

Red, White, and Blue

MATERIALS: Navy star paper • Red sequin mesh • Gold star • Navy Blue marker

INSTRUCTIONS:
Adhere Red sequin mesh. • Apply Gold foil to the cap. • Edge the star sticker with a Navy Blue marker. • Adhere sticker and Gold star to the tag.

Ho Ho Ho

MATERIALS: Santas paper • Gold stars

INSTRUCTIONS:
Add Gold stars. • Apply Gold foil to a Navy Blue bottle cap. • Cut the word "HO" from bottle cap stickers and adhere to the tag and bottle cap.

Jingle Bells

MATERIALS: Gift wrap (Music paper, Green) • Krylon Gold Leaf pen • Ranger Antique Linen Distress ink

INSTRUCTIONS:
Add a strip of music paper and a Red cap. • Age the sticker with Distress ink. • Apply a sticker to the cap. • Make a small bow and glue it above the bottle cap. • Edge tag with the Gold leaf pen.

'Tis the Season

MATERIALS: Papers: Red Holly, Green Holly • Krylon Gold Foil pen

INSTRUCTIONS:
Cut papers to fit on tag making it half Green and half Red. • Glue a piece of ribbon down the center seam. • Flatten a bottle cap. Apply a sticker. Edge the bottle cap with Gold pen.

Christmas

MATERIALS: Papers: Diamonds with Holly, Christmas • Ranger Antique Linen Distress ink • ColorBox Metalextra Gold Rush

INSTRUCTIONS:
Cut out the word "Christmas" from the Christmas paper. Add a sticker and the cut-out "Christmas". • Apply ink onto the tag. • Apply Gold foil to bottle cap.

Gift Tags

by Judy Claxton

Make a handful of these fun tags in an hour and you will have plenty when you need them. Gift tags also make a nice present for the hostess of the holiday party!

GENERAL MATERIALS: Bottle Caps: Navy Blue, Green, Red • Stickers: Holiday Sayings, Patriotic • 2½" square tag • Gold leafing supplies • Gold leafing pen• Gold foil • Tack iron • Ribbon or fibers • E6000 adhesive • Glue stick

INSTRUCTIONS:
Cover the tag with decorative paper. • Attach bottle caps to tags with E6000 glue. • Add ribbon or fiber to the hole to finish the tag. • Gold Foil. Tip: Apply Gold leaf adhesive along the edge of tag. Let dry. • Add foil to the edge with a tap iron.

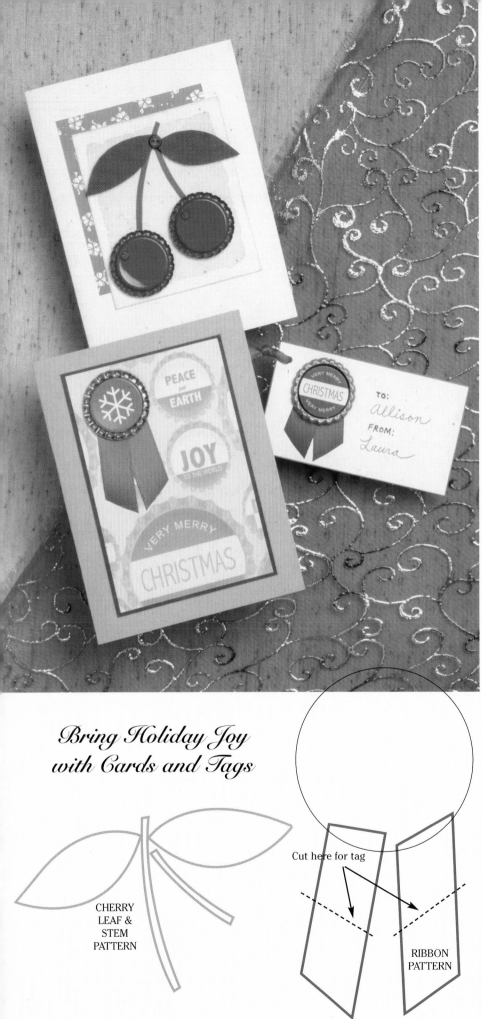

Cherries Card

by Molly Jennings

Send this summertime cherry card to someone you love and celebrate the sweetness of life.

MATERIALS: Cardstock: Confetti White, Dark Green • Decorative paper: Red, White • 2 Red Bottle Caps • Green craft foam • 2 Red rhinestones • *Tsukineko* Encore Metallic Gold ink • *Hero Arts* (tiny Green button, Shadow stamp) • Glue

INSTRUCTIONS:

Card: Cut Confetti cardstock 5½" x 8½". • Fold card to 4¼" x 5½". • Cut a mat 3" x 3½" from both Red and White paper. • Stamp the Shadow design with light coat of Gold ink on the White mat. • Brush the edges with the Gold ink. • Overlap the mats and glue in place.

Accents: Cut stems from Green cardstock. • Cut leaves from foam. • Flatten 2 bottle caps. • Glue stems, caps, and leaves in place. • Add a rhinestone to each cherry. Add a button over leaves.

Christmas Card

by Molly Jennings

This simple, attractive card gets its charm from the Christmas paper. It coordinates beautifully with the tan card and the bottle cap embellishment.

MATERIALS: Christmas paper • Cardstock: Tan, Green • Gold Bottle Cap • Holiday Sayings sticker • ⅝" wide Red satin ribbon • Glue

INSTRUCTIONS:

Card: Cut Tan cardstock 5½" x 8½". • Fold card to 4¼" x 5½". • Cut a Green mat 3¼" x 4¾". Adhere to the card. • Cut a Christmas paper mat 3⅛" x 4⅝". • Glue it to the card.

Accents: Flatten the bottle cap. • Adhere the sticker. • Cut two pieces of ribbon 2" long and glue it in place. • Glue the cap over the ribbon.

Christmas Tag

by Molly Jennings

Happy Christmas to all, and to all a Good Night! It will be a good night when you can relax and enjoy it because you made your gift tags in advance.

MATERIALS: Confetti White cardstock • Silver Bottle Cap • Holiday Sayings sticker • Red satin ribbon widths (⅝", ³⁄₁₆") • Markers: Red, fine point Black • Hole punch • Glue

INSTRUCTIONS:

Flatten the bottle cap. • Cut out a 2" x 4" Confetti tag. • Draw around edges with a Red marker. • Punch a hole in the corner. • Add a narrow ribbon with a Lark's head knot. • Cut 2 wide ribbons 1" long and glue to card. • Glue the cap over the ribbons. • Place a Christmas sticker inside the cap. • Write "To" and "From" on the tag with a Black marker.

Bring Holiday Joy with Cards and Tags

CHERRY LEAF & STEM PATTERN

Cut here for tag

RIBBON PATTERN

MATERIALS: Bottle Caps: 2 Red, 4 White • Holiday Sayings stickers • 3 Snowflake foam shapes • Gold elastic cord • Brush on glitter: Gold, Silver, Green, Blue • E6000 adhesive

INSTRUCTIONS:
Apply Blue glitter to both sides of snowflakes. Let dry. • Apply stickers and glitter to caps. Let dry. • Add a Gold cord to each snowflake. • Adhere caps to both sides of snowflakes.

Snowflake Ornaments
by Gail Ellspermann

Let it Snow! These lovely snowflakes are beautiful as ornaments and decorations on gifts. Have even more fun by turning them into a mobile or hang them in the window. This is also an easy project for the kids to make for teacher gifts or the cub scout fundraiser.

SNOWFLAKE
PATTERN

Christmas Tree Card
by Michele Charles

Bottle caps can be used to make so many holiday motifs - holly berries, snowflakes and trees!

MATERIALS: Manila cardstock • Bottle Caps: 1 Red, 6 Green • Red Alphabet stickers • *Prismacolor* pencils: Red, Green • *Marvy* Green marker • Holly stamp • Black ink • The Ultimate! glue

INSTRUCTIONS:
Cut cardstock 6" x 8½". Fold to 4¼" x 6". • Edge the card front with a Green marker.
• Stamp 6 holly leaves and color with pencils. • Cut out holly leaves and glue them to bottle caps. • Glue caps to the card in a tree shape. • Glue Red cap for the tree trunk. • Spell "Merry" with Red Alphabet stickers.

Wreath

by Michele Charles

An icon of welcome and celebration, this wreath is decorated with cut-outs from decorative paper.

MATERIALS: Diamonds with Holly paper • Ivory cardstock • Ivory paper • 7 Gold Bottle Caps • Green organza ribbon • Rubber stamps (*JudiKins* Snowflake background, Merry Christmas) • Ink (*Marvy* Cherry Red; *Tsukineko* Brilliance Galaxy Gold) • Metallic Gold marker • Red paint • Heat gun • The Ultimate! glue

INSTRUCTIONS:

Card: Cut Ivory cardstock to 7" x 10". Fold in half to 5" x 7". • Paint the card front Red. Let dry. • Stamp snowflake background with Gold ink. Heat set. • Edge the card front with the Gold marker.

Accents: Cut out holly images from Diamonds with Holly paper. • Glue a holly image to each bottle cap. • Glue the caps in a circle shape to the front of card. • Tie a small bow with Green organza ribbon and glue it to the base of the wreath. • Stamp a Christmas phrase in Cherry Red ink on Ivory paper. • Tear around edges and glue it to card front.

Child's Christmas

by Michele Charles

If you prefer the nostalgic Victorian style for giving, you are going to love a Child's Christmas.

MATERIALS: Paper: Diamonds with Holly, Green Linen • Ivory cardstock • 3 Red Bottle Caps • Holiday Sayings stickers • Dictionary slide mount • Holidays 2 Transparency • *ColorBox* ink: Scarlet, Brown • Heat gun • The Ultimate! glue

INSTRUCTIONS:

Card: Cut cardstock to 5" x 10" and fold to 5" x 5". • Glue Green Linen paper to the card front. • Tear a corner of the Diamonds with Holly paper and edge with Scarlet and Brown inks. • Glue it to the lower left corner of card front.

Mount: Ink the mount with Scarlet and Brown. Heat set. • Glue the transparency image to the mount. • Glue a White paper mat to the back of the mount. • Glue the mount to the front of the card.

Accents: Cut 2 holly images from the Diamonds with Holly paper. • Flatten the bottle caps. Adhere a sticker to a cap. • Glue the holly images to the other caps. Glue the caps to the front of card.

Santa

by Michele Charles

'Tis the season to wish you a happy holiday! Santa comes to town in a delightful bottle cap card.

MATERIALS: Christmas paper • Large Window card • Large White slide mount • Holidays 2 Transparency • Bottle Caps: 2 Red, 1 Green • Holiday Sayings stickers • *ColorBox* Evergreen ink • Craft knife • Heat gun • The Ultimate! glue

INSTRUCTIONS:

Card: Cover the card front with Christmas paper. • Cut the paper from window. • Ink the edge of the card with Evergreen.

Mount: Color the mount with Evergreen ink and heat set. • Glue the Santa transparency image to the mount.